"No student of American Jewish writing needs to be [illegible] that Jules Chametzky is one of its pioneers. . . . He now caps a distinguished career as critic, editor, and teacher with this delightful volume of memoirs."

—Joseph C. Landis, editor of
Yiddish-Modern Jewish Studies

"A raconteur's timing and wit leaven the author's perceptive literary intelligence. This combination is so seductive, the stories so entertaining and engrossing that we only gradually come to recognize how gracefully we have been ushered into serious literary history."

—Michael Thelwell,
Daily Hampshire Gazette

Out of Brownsville

Out of Brownsville:
Encounters with Nobel Laureates and Other Jewish Writers

A Cultural Memoir

By Jules Chametzky

UNIVERSITY OF MASSACHUSETTS PRESS
Amherst and Boston

Originally published by Meredith Winter Press,
Cambridge, Massachusetts, 2012.
First paperback edition published by
University of Massachusetts Press, 2013.

Library of Congress Control Number: 2013945199
ISBN 978-1-62534-036-8

Printed and bound by Gasch Printing, LLC.

Legendary editor Jules Chametzky's book is autobiography at its cleanest: one's life through the eyes of others. His astute, personable dispatches are a map of Jewish intellectual trends in the United States in the second half of the twentieth century.

ILAN STAVANS

Table of Contents

Foreword

The editors of *The Massachusetts Review*, the journal I helped to found in 1958–59, and of which I have been editor, emeritus, since 2002, devoted an issue to Grace Paley, some months after her death, and asked me to contribute some words. I wrote a one-page tribute that the editors thought good enough to publish, so I sent a copy to my sons, who responded with the welcomed filial praise. One of my sons, Peter, went a step further and suggested I put together some forty or fifty such pieces, some a bit longer, and perhaps talk somewhat about the work of these writers, too. He knew I had met or known—some fleetingly, a few more intensely—and over fifty years had written about many writers, and that I often had a story or anecdote about each. Forty or fifty pieces! I thought that was wildly exaggerated. Then I began making lists, stopping when I reached a hundred names. Obviously, I would have to do some pruning. In light of much of my professional interests, especially in recent years, I decided to focus on Jewish writers I had encountered and who had made some kind of memorable impression upon me. That number approached seventy. So here we are—from that number I winnowed down to the present contents. I began my selections with my origins in Brooklyn, specifically the fertile literary and social ground of its Brownsville section, although our family also lived for several years in Williamsburg and Crown Heights. After leaving Brooklyn I moved on to the University of Minnesota, where I did my graduate work, married, taught, began a family; then back east to Boston and finally Amherst at the University of Massachusetts, with visits along the way to universities and other venues in Europe. A lot of reading and talking ensued over these years, but most memorably, I met a varied and enriching number of writers, artists, and intellectuals. I have been fortunate, indeed, and I would like to share some of that good fortune in the following pages.

A model and influence for what I hope to achieve with these small personal, perhaps idiosyncratic, comments, essays, *obiter dicta*, is a work by the international journalist Clive James called *Cultural Amnesia* (2007). In that encyclopedic book, James tries to vivify works and writers from all of Western literature of the past century, often writers and works that most of us don't know or have forgotten. Taken together, however, they represent a civilization. Valuable, instructive, and at the same time entertaining.

My ambition is not that large and my writers not that foreign to us, or at least they should not be. I don't pretend to have been an intimate of those I will remember, nor will I discuss their work in detail. Over the years I have written about many of them, in journal articles and reviews, in popular and scholarly formats, about some not at all. But each has touched me, and with each I had a memorable meeting or with some a longer connection and more encounters.

Taken together these experiences, these writers, have

helped me to understand my times and myself. These bits and pieces, and the larger corpus of work for which they stand comprise a mosaic of a culture—Jewish American literati and literature within the larger framework of an American literature and culture that stretches over half a century. My hope is that some small insights, illuminations, and pleasure emanating from these pieces may help rescue that culture from the memory hole of time, for those who care, and from the cultural amnesia that should concern us all.

Acknowledgments

I would like to thank Jack Polidori and Eva Peterson, Joann Kobin, Jim Hicks, Mike Thelwell, Bruce Laurie and many other good friends who have read and supported this work in whole or part. Very special thanks to Julia Meyerson, brilliant and tireless editor of the Meredith Winter Press, and to its gracious and generous publisher. The work is dedicated to my late wife Anne Halley, who shared many of the experiences and the life recounted in this work.

Several of these pieces have appeared over the past two years in *The Massachusetts Review*, *Yiddish*, and the JewDayo blog of *Jewish Currents*. We thank their editors for permission to reprint them.

Alfred Kazin

I owe Kazin. In *A Walker in the City* he wrote about walking the same Brownsville streets I had walked; learned Civics from the same crazy (he called him "roguish") teacher at Lew Wallace Junior High No. 66; dreamed the same dream of crossing over to the real City across the river. That book opened up and made available our whole world of second generation Jewish American life, changed my life—as did I. B. Singer, Isaac Rosenfeld, even Norman Podhoretz—but Kazin was the first and closest to me.

For twenty-five years my father owned a kosher butcher shop on Belmont Avenue, a street Kazin called "the great open street market," which he loved for its liveliness, as I did, and the "open, hearty" market women (and men) who hawked their wares in loud, triumphant voices:

> "*Vayber! Vayber! Sheyne gute vayber!* Oh you lovelies! Oh you good ones! Oh you pretty ones! See how cheap and good! Just come over! Just taste! Just a little look! What will it cost you to taste? How can you walk on without looking? How can you resist us? Oh! Oh! Come over! Devour us! Storm us! Tear us apart! BARGAINS! BARGAINS!"

When I showed this passage to my mother, who helped out in the store three days a week—the calm, gentle one the customers loved, rather than my irascible father smoking his Lucky Strikes, preferring to read *Der Tog*—she said the herring and pickle man two stores down had stopped that kind of hawking. So she then showed the passage to him, and, *annus mirabilis*, he began doing it again, trying for word for word fidelity to the text!

I met Kazin at an American Studies meeting and told him this story, and of course he, like I, pondered the power of art. Taken from life, then influencing life. But he was suspicious when I said that as a teenager I had been friends with Podhoretz, coming from the same neighborhood (we had moved from the depths of Brownsville to the higher status Ocean Hill-Brownsville). "But you lived on St. Marks Avenue, and he lived on Pacific Street!" I pointed out that those streets were only two blocks apart, and that we played ball in the same schoolyard; nevertheless, I suspected he regarded me as some kind of impostor, an *arriviste* to those sacred grounds.

I owed him in other crucial ways. My wife, Anne Halley, had taken his course at Minnesota, where he was a temporary guest professor, the year before I arrived there. The other grad students, New Criticism wannabes, disdained Kazin's emotional, engaged humanism, the catch in his throat when he read Whitman aloud—to them, "non-U" in that snobbish time. Anne responded warmly to his uncomplicated love of literature, and his simple, democratic manner. When she hadn't finished her term paper before his permanent departure for New York, he called her up, asked her to read what she had written, and gave her an A. In effect he opened the way for me, another Brownsville boy, as Anne chose a few years later to be with me (for fifty-two years) instead of other perfectly nice and accomplished suitors who had asked to marry her.

I owe him much—which makes the revelation in his former wife Ann Birstein's book, *What I Saw at the Fair*, so disturbing. At the end of that interesting book about New York intellectual life in the late forties and fifties, and the writing of *A Walker in the City*, in which she played an important part, she reveals that Alfred was physically abusive—he beat her. I am still shocked as I write these words. I know and admire Ann, and we have had good times together at various occasions. She is an attractive, very intelligent woman, and a fine writer. I had always admired Kazin, his fine reviews, *On Native Grounds*, of course, his liberality, his refusal to go along with the conservative turn of so many of his friends and contemporaries—sticking to his humanistic guns. And then this dirty little secret? What to make of it? Am I naïve?

I had to go back to re-read his 1978 book, *New York Jew*, the third and beautifully written memoir in the series that began with *A Walker in the City*. In this later work he presents richly detailed accounts of his life among the New York intellectuals, his career at *The New Republic* and *Time/Life* under Henry Luce (an extraordinary portrait of the man and the publications), and evocative accounts of the war and post-war years in the United States and in various western European countries. Moreover, Kazin writes honestly about his sexual awakenings and loves during those years, and of his three marriages. Among these, his second marriage, to Ann, whom he calls "Beth" in the book, gets a good deal of attention. He seems to face up to the many difficulties and joys in that relationship, including bouts of "violent quarrels," fueled by drinking, so common in those times, especially among intellectuals and, in my experience, academics in literary departments.

One can at first assume that the violence may only have been "verbal abuse," even though it occasionally involved throwing dishes at one another—perhaps a deliberate ambiguity on Kazin's part. One of Birstein's claims in a different but important matter is that Kazin did not give her credit for her working over and helping him write every page of *A Walker in the City*, which he composed while living with her. In *New York Jew* he does say she went over every line of that seminal work with him, in one of New York's cafeterias (a credible touch about that time and place!) It may be that he was correcting the oversight Birstein had charged him with. Is her charge of physical abuse overstated? It remains hard to say, though probably not.

Whatever the final truth, it remains a disturbing allegation.

In a sense, I suppose it goes with the times, though still present among all classes of people, and lately we have learned about the abuse of wives in Hasidic and ultra-Orthodox circles. But I am still shocked and puzzled. My father would storm out of the house in anger at times, returning when he had cooled off; my patriarchal *zayde*, imperious lifetime president of his small *shtiebel shul* in Williamsburg; and his father Yitzhok, who bragged of beating Russian gendarmes in his early days—I could not imagine any of them, or Tevye the Milkman, raising an arm in anger at their wives. For one thing, they were all married to strong women, who could and would give as good as they took, despite the supposed subordinate role of women in traditional Judaism. It just didn't go with the territory. For our generation I wonder if in crossing over to the City, going from the village to the Village, our generation's Americanization may have had some deep flaws in it. Alfred Kazin should have dealt with that, too, "The Woman Question," in all its complexity and power, as he so often did, brilliantly, with so many of the other fulfillments and disappointments in that process.

Norman Podhoretz

*Normie Pod is **blatt** [cool],*
but I'll take Billie Bernstein—
seven seasons in the mountains under his belt;
*Normie's got the schooling, but Billie's got the **gelt!***

T hus the neighborhood bard's song, the rhythm banged out on the newsstand in front of the perennial candy store that was the center of social and communal life for boys in the 'hood during the thirties until shortly after World War II. That was on Pacific Street in Ocean Hill-Brownsville. We were in our teens, down the street from the school that was to erupt in a near riot in 1968 between the by-then black residents and the schoolteachers over the issue of neighborhood control of the schools. It was the occasion, among other events, for one of Podhoretz's best known and perhaps incendiary pieces, "My Negro Problem—and Ours." In the essay, he admits to admiring always the superior athletic abilities of the black players in that schoolyard, where we all played basketball, and to his basic fear of them too. His solution to America's apparently intractable race "problem" was intermarriage, over time, etc. etc. When I read the piece, my first thought was that Normie was envious of all the ballplayers, white and black, since he never was much of an athlete. Now

I wonder what he feels, besides fear and envy, about that pretty good black ballplayer in the White House.

The doggerel above, remembered all these years since, was a mock celebration of money over brains—Billie B. did go on from his years of waiting on tables in the mountains to become an accountant, of course—but everyone really admired Norman's superior intellect. Both of us had started college (he at Columbia and I at Brooklyn); he was reading Eliot's "Wasteland" while I was deep into Dalton Trumbo's *Johnny Got His Gun*—a foreshadowing, no doubt, of where our futures would take us. We talked a lot, about politics—he was a solid Democrat, along with about 97 percent of all the Jews in New York, while I was veering left—and Judaism, about which he influenced me positively. Academically talented and ambitious, he was going for a degree at night at the Jewish Theological Seminary as well as attending Columbia.

Having broken away completely from my family's Orthodoxy, after a philosophy course in college that shredded any lingering belief in the supernatural, I was nevertheless willing to give Judaism and religion one more try. He suggested I go to the Seminary School of Jewish Studies, which I did, taking two courses. Though it did not make me any more observant, alas, it did teach me a few things, especially about Jewish literature in a class with Rabbi Louis Gerstein of the Spanish and Portuguese Synagogue in Manhattan, starting with the *Pirke Aboth*. That has stood me in good stead as I went on to teach and write about, among other things, Jewish and Yiddish literature.

Norman went off to Clare College, Cambridge on a two-year scholarship, where he reacted strongly to the strains of anti-Americanism during the Korean War, as I was told by one of his leftish British classmates there (who had come to Minnesota for a year), perhaps the beginning of his move to the right. That did not happen immediately. He came back and worked for *The New Yorker*, writing to me about that strange collection of people. He also chided me, not altogether incorrectly, about getting into "Talmudic Faulknerism," because at the time I was editing, though still a graduate student, a small journal called *Faulkner Studies*. Podhoretz, who was by then an assistant editor at *Commentary*, earned me points in the Humanities Department at Minnesota when he came looking for me on his way to St. Paul to meet his fiancée Midge Decter's family. I was not around the department just then and never did meet Midge Decter, except very briefly, until many years later. Pod had also written to me about the inner struggles at *Commentary*. The well-known long-time editor was in a psychiatric facility on Long Island for what promised to be a long time, while pretenders to the throne maneuvered for the job. Norman emerged, finally, as editor towards the end of the fifties and beginning of the sixties. The rest, as they say, is history.

He wrote some fine essays in the fifties, such as "The Know-Nothing Bohemians," and "The New Nihilism," for *Partisan Review* and elsewhere, attacking the emerging Beat movement and the growing cult around Kerouac's *On the Road*. I agreed with much of it, though I don't think he appreciated or understood sufficiently the currents in America's cultural and economic life, especially as they appeared to the young, the marginal, the oppressed. The Beats presaged a revolt against the conventions and reigning assumptions in American life of the 1950s that appeared to make a satisfying emotional life difficult. In the early sixties, Podhoretz did publish Paul Goodman and Norman Mailer in *Commentary*, whose antennae were more attuned to those currents. But then came the frightful escalation of the Vietnam War, and that's when Norman took a sharp turn towards the conservatism that fathered the terrible neo-con empowerment and its disastrous consequences.

How exactly did that happen? Here's one theory, which I developed after a conversation with William Phillips during the time we were working together as officers of the Coordinating Council of Literary Magazines (CCLM) from 1967 to 1972. Podhoretz had come out with *Making It*, the book in which he thought he had laid bare his soul and the "dirty little secret" of American life—that it was good to succeed, make money, not be a loser. For there he was, at the end of the book, enjoying a drink at poolside with Jason Epstein, celebrating their good fortune on a Caribbean Island. He thought he would be admired for his honesty. Instead, given the tenor of the time, the horrible war and the draft, people, especially the young, thought, "Who is this guy? Is he kidding?" I ended a review of some other book in an academic journal at the time with a gratuitous swipe at that ending—I asked, rhetorically, what would Tolstoy say about that? Was that the aim and purpose of life? Phillips said Norman wouldn't like me saying that. What? It's in an obscure little journal, he'll never see it. "He'll see it," was William's laconic response. About then, too, Lyndon Johnson invited him to the White House, and jawboned him in his inimitable fashion for forty-five minutes, I believe, and Norman came out an ardent defender of the War. And all that followed.

By the early seventies we were no longer friends. We mumbled a quick hello one afternoon, meeting by chance outside Zabar's. Some time later, at the 50th anniversary of *Partisan Review,* celebrated at the Century Club in Manhattan, he arrived with Irving Kristol and John Silber, the egregious president of Boston University, who was then the patron of *Partisan*—"the princes of darkness," the *Village Voice* reporter standing next to me said. I received barely a nod. At a humanities conference at Yale in which we both participated, on different panels, in the eighties, we didn't speak at all. He was loudly booed by that audience—the only time I experienced such a thing at an academic affair. Most recently, however, we met at the memorial service for William Phillips at the Ethical Culture Society, and we spoke, perhaps because we had both contributed to the 2003 *Partisan Review* tribute to Phillips, who had died the year before. I was introduced to Midge, who was actually sociable, seemed genuinely glad to meet me "at last," as she said. What does that mean? Has he mellowed (I doubt it), or have I?

Hi, Normie!

Isaac Bashevis Singer

The last time I met Singer was towards the end of his life, in his residence hotel in Miami Beach, not far from the upscale Bal Harbor Mall that his wife Alma visited every day. I was in Miami for the month of January, 1989, working on a long essay covering most of Singer's life and oeuvre for a new *HarperCollins Reader's Encyclopedia of American Literature* and had arranged for an interview through Alma. She had assented when I reminded her of our earlier meetings and my several pieces about his work since the early 1960s. So Anne—my wife Anne Halley—and I waited in the lobby at the assigned hour for Singer and Alma to come down from their apartment. They came, Isaac in a wheelchair, attended by a Spanish-speaking nurse. I had not realized until then that one of the reasons for their now permanent residence in Florida was the availability of the twenty-four hour care he required.

After our greetings, he surprised me with his first comment: "You interviewed me before, when you were making that movie!" Uncomprehendingly, I started to correct this idea, never having made a movie in my life (in the early 1950s I did write the narrative for a Jerome Liebling documentary on Red Lake Minnesota Indians), when it suddenly occurred to me that my name was close, in a way, to someone else's who *had* made a movie based on a Singer novel. "No," I said, "that was Paul Mazursky, who made *Enemies*, a very good movie, Mazursky's best, I would say." Another connection that of course Singer couldn't have known about, and that frankly was only of personal interest, was that Mazursky and I had lived around the corner from each other in Ocean Hill-Brownsville and were at Brooklyn College at the same time, where he was a very talented actor named Irwin Mazursky. A perhaps apocryphal story, more like a Jewish joke, about why he changed his first name is that in Hollywood "Mazursky" sounded too Jewish, so he changed from "Irwin" to "Paul." I told this story to Singer, who then seemed momentarily confused by Mazursky's two first names and slumped somewhat sadly back in his chair. The interview proceeded fitfully for no more than fifteen to twenty minutes, mostly monosyllabically, illuminated once or twice by a sharply phrased insight, or even a Biblical reference, that recalled an earlier Singer.

The Isaac Bashevis Singer of an earlier time I met in 1981 at a reception and dinner at the home of our provost at the University of Massachusetts Amherst, after a talk Singer had presented there, under the auspices of an institute I directed. Singer had given an impish performance, including some murky reflections on the mysteries and unknowns of a world of forces in which, for example, our clothing often crackled with static electricity. Was he putting us on? One never knew—and in light of his extraordinary stories and books, it really didn't matter. The list of all his wonderful works would be a chapter in itself. My favorites, among many—including "Gimpel the Fool," of course, Saul Bellow's translation of which, when published in *Partisan Review* in 1953, was the occasion for

Singer's breakthrough into the literary mainstream—are *Satan in Goray*, "The Seance," and *Slaves*.

That last, I was told by Ted Hughes at a dinner party in Devon given by Lisa and Leonard Baskin, had just been published in England and had enraptured the English literary establishment. Seated next to me, Hughes broke the ice by asking who I believed was the best living American writer. I offered Faulkner. No. Bellow? No. Hughes thought Singer was the greatest living American writer. Our conversation went swimmingly after that.

In any case, Singer's performance that evening in Amherst does remind one of his sometimes perverse side. In his later fame he sometimes played the benign *zayde*, but he could also be the tricky and foxy grandpa. There is the oft-repeated story, perhaps only academic folklore, about his request before a lecture to thousands at Northrup Auditorium in Minneapolis, that it would help to have someone ask a question prepared beforehand. One of the eminent professors at the pre-speech dinner volunteered. What should he ask? "Ask me how my work and Marc Chagall's are alike." After Singer's presentation, the professor stood up and asked the first question. Singer's response: "Vot a stupid question!" I have mercifully omitted the name of that unfortunate questioner.

But Singer was in a good mood at our reception. When my turn came to shake his hand and introduce myself, he smiled (a very sweet smile in that innocent-looking *yeshiva bocher's* pale face) and said, "Ah, Chametzky!" But he pronounced the "Ch" like the Hebrew letter "Khometz"—a guttural, rasping sound. "Ah, Khometzky, I like what you write about me." I surmised he may have referred to a piece I did in *The Nation* in 1966, easily available at New York newsstands, unlike other work in academic journals. I laughed. A bit put out, he asked why I laughed at that. I said I hadn't been called "Khometzky since Kheder!" He smiled again.

Some years earlier, the first time I actually met Singer, in the late sixties, he had spoken at Smith College and Leonard Baskin, then a professor of art at Smith, invited him to his house afterward. There, Leonard and his wife Lisa, Rabbi Yechiel Lander and his wife Rose, and Anne and I spent several hours in warm and easy talk, Singer obviously pleased with the elegant Baskin home. Leonard had long been a champion of Singer's writing, inviting Cecil Helmley, one of Singer's earliest translators and publishers, to his home after a talk at Amherst College, and he and I had attempted a translation of two Singer stories from the *Forverts* for possible publication in *The Massachusetts Review*. Leonard had designed the format of the journal at its inception and edited its art sections for four years. We had given up on the translation project for two reasons: one, the Yiddish was too hard, with many vernacular Polish words included—for example, the word for the slop bucket under a sink, which I had to ask my mother to translate for me; and two, the stories contained unabashed anti-Christian sentiments that we thought might be too explosive in the early and precarious days of our journal.

I recall especially Singer's stories about the *Forverts* and its famous editor, Abraham Cahan. I had begun work on a book about Cahan's fiction, and so primed the pump of Singer's reminiscences. He and Cahan never really got along.

The realist Cahan always distrusted the quasi-mystical, sometimes demon-haunted side of Singer's work, hiring him in the mid-thirties only because of I. J. Singer, Isaac's older brother, a formidable and famous realist writer of epic books that Cahan admired fulsomely. So he told stories about Cahan's meanness. Such as: There was a very short subeditor on the newspaper, very, very short, and lame. Leaving work one day, he looked about frantically for his cane, which appeared to be missing. Annoyed, Cahan turned to him and snapped, "Never mind the cane, here, use a pencil!"

Then, too, Singer had an irreverent attitude towards the newspaper itself (not nice of him, considering the years it was his only publisher and means of support, however meager), especially in the years of its waning glory and influence. The editors thought they needed to keep themselves and their readers up on modern science. So every Monday, as Singer told it, they carefully read the science stories in the Sunday *Times*, which they translated into Yiddish, the assigned writer usually adding a personal note to make it seem like his work. In writing about the sun, the center of our solar system, on one occasion, the writer reported on the sun's diameter and circumference, and the heat generated on the outer surface, say a million degrees Fahrenheit; in the center of the earth, about a billion degrees. "And there," wrote the writer, pausing to add his personal note, "it was really hot."

God bless you, Isaac Bashevis (a pseudonym he often used in the *Forverts*), With love, Khometzky

Morty Gunty

Woody Allen's movie *Broadway Danny Rose* opens in the Carnegie Deli, where four old-time Jewish Borscht Belt comedians are sitting around a table, reminiscing about the fictional character Danny Rose, an unusual agent with a heart. I recognized two of them. Morty Gunty starred in my first play as a student at Brooklyn College. The other was Jackie Mason, whom I said hello to once or twice at the bar of the Fontainebleau in Miami Beach years ago, where my wife and I often went for a drink after working out at the gym, and to talk with the regular old Haitian bartender. I never liked Mason's type of humor, which I found vulgar and exploitative, at least in our era, with its faux Yinglish, and what used to be called in the days of the Yiddish theatre *schundliteratur*, trashy literature which basically panders to Jewish stereotypes. Even if, in its possible defense, it occasionally undercuts those stereotypes.

I love good Jewish humor, being exposed to it full time when I was an assistant stage manager at Sha-Wan-Ga Lodge ("66 Miles From New York, Why Go Further?" was its road sign greeting) for six weeks in the summer of 1949, towards the last gasp of that wonderful institution, "the mountains." Sha-Wan-Ga (called by its staff "Schvenga"—Yiddish for "Pregnancy"—Lodge) may have been the inspiration for Arthur Kober's 1930s play *Having Wonderful Time*, which

16

became the musical *Wish You Were Here*. The Lodge was also the site, it was claimed by the management, true or false, of a well-known 1936 Rodgers and Hart song, "There's a Small Hotel, By a Wishing Well." Part of my job was to put ice around that well at 6 a.m. every morning to ensure that the guests were getting good, cold mountain water. For the comedians I swept the stage in the Casino and lifted the curtain for the best and the worst—the best humor being like the blues, an instrument for dulling the edge of pain ("Why am I so black and blue?") and creating beauty out of it, as in the work of Myron Cohen and Sam Levenson, Phil Foster, many others. Cohen wowed them with his stories of the garment center and its tribulations. "Business was so bad Jack jumped out of the window of his shop the other day." "What! I didn't know he killed himself." "No, no, he landed on a pile of returns." But as business continued to go downhill and his shop came to a standstill, he jumped again. As he fell he looked into the window of the shop below his and saw two hundred machines busily at work. With his last breath he yelled up to his partner, "Morris, cut velvet!" The audiences ate it up.

Levenson was more gentle, a feel-good storyteller, a Jewish Garrison Keillor, ahead of his time. His grandfather loved *kishke* (stuffed *derma*), he said, highly peppered, which he ingested into his *kishkes* (his intestines), the heartburn keeping him warm through the Russian winters. Reminiscent of Buddy Hackett, who said that when he was in the Army and ate only non-Jewish food, which did not give him heartburn, he thought his fire had gone out. When Levenson went on stage, this former Spanish teacher turned to my boss standing in the wings, who was a high school teacher in the offseason, mocking him, "You school-teacher you, what do you know about managing a stage?" And they both laughed, fellow conspirators, getting away with it. I think we all felt that, to a degree, and not just about the stage. (These jokes and many others can be found in my essay, "Jewish Humor," in *Jewish American Literature: A Norton Anthology* [2001], that I co-edited with great pleasure and pride.)

The worst was a twitchy fellow of little original talent named Jack Roy, né Jacob Cohen, who was a temporary June replacement for our regular M.C. The regular for many seasons was a wonderful burlesque comic named Sammy Smith, who came with a trunkful of the old routines that we rehearsed on the ball-field (The Hunky-Dory Ice Cream Peddler: "Niagara Falls! Slowly, I turned...") and performed twice a week. Roy got no respect from us and we enjoyed teasing him for his lack of original material—we accused him of stealing from Phil Foster, who would punish him when he arrived for his turn. He suffered silently. Some years later I was watching TV with my sons, and I said of the new comedian on the small screen, "I know that guy!" Of course it was Rodney Dangerfield, who had transformed himself yet again, in name and routine. He had put his neurosis to work in a positive way. With "I don't get no respect," he became the top headliner of his day, an everyman of woes and sorrows whom one had to love as we laughed at and with him.

Morty Gunty was different. He never became a headliner but worked regularly at gigs until the end of his days—which occurred shortly after the Woody Allen film. Gunty was very much like the central character in Billy Crystal's fine film rendition of that lost world of *tummlers* and Jewish entertainers, *Mr. Saturday Night*. Morty had starred in my college comedy, the details of which I will mercifully spare you, very much in the style of Jerry Lewis, popular then and not just in France, hamming it up and whining nasally through the script. He acted a lot at Brooklyn College, as did Irwin (Paul) Mazursky, who did a brilliant Cyrano de Bergerac there. Mazursky went on to fame and fortune, as did a few others in that cohort, but not Morty. At our graduation, he asked me to write comedy material for him as he prepared to go professional. Surprised, I said, "But I can't write comedy routines, life makes me too sad most of the time." His riposte was accurate: "What do you think most of us are?" Yes, there is a strain of melancholy through much of Jewish humor, certainly in Woody Allen's work, but it is full, too, of wonder and joy as mirth breaks through, offering us pleasure as we learn in our guts and the deep regions of our brains about the resilience of the human spirit.

Howard Sackler
& Friend

At the Christmas break after my first quarter of graduate school in Minnesota, I returned to New York and almost immediately visited my old haunts in Greenwich Village. Outside one of the bars, I unexpectedly ran into Howard Sackler, who had been a classmate of mine at Brooklyn College the year before. We were in a small class on eighteenth-century literature, given by Professor Morris Roberts, who turned out to be the most impressive teacher I had at the College. I had had excellent, inspiring teachers—Frederick Ewen and Harry Slochower, Marxists who breathed the air of a broader world into their Modern and World Literature classes, and Bernard Grebanier, an anti-Communist who had testified against some of his colleagues during the Rapp-Coudert investigation, but whose line by line explication of *Romeo and Juliet*, *Hamlet*, and *King Lear* in his Shakespeare course were extraordinary. But Roberts was the only one whose probity and accuracy held up through graduate school and beyond; nothing he ever said was proven wrong or even seriously debatable. He gave me a B, not a bad grade in those days, although the others endowed me with As, which proves how smart he was! Sackler was the star of the class, he and Professor Roberts talking to each other about those arcane poets in ways the rest of us could never manage, only marvel at.

Sackler was a poet, who was already friendly, while only an undergraduate, with W. H. Auden, to whom he showed and who liked his work. What also impressed me was his wonderful wavy blonde hair and a huge ring he wore on a long dangling finger. Envying his style and savoir-faire, I knew he would go far—and indeed, his play *The Great White Hope* was a terrific piece of work, the film with James Earl Jones as the renowned black boxer Jack Johnson and Jane Alexander as his white mistress a vehicle for two great performances as well as a powerful assault on the great American sin/tragedy of racism. At the time I wasn't aware he had that in him, but the liberal air of Brooklyn College apparently had an effect on him as well as those others of us lucky enough to have been there then. But that night in the Village his success was years away. So what was he up to, I asked.

"Well," he said, "I'm about to go to Mexico to make a movie I'll help to write. Some of the people from Brooklyn are going too and will be in it." Really? I said. Several of the people he named I had known and worked with in my days as an undergraduate playwright. I thought it was a kind of pipe dream, a fantasy that we all indulged in at one time or another. Why didn't he go to graduate school instead, I thought, much more realistic. "Who's going to pay for all that?" I dared to say, instead. "Well, the director and producer is a fellow who was a photographer for *Look* magazine; he's giving up a $10,000 a year job to do it." That got my attention: to us in 1950 a sum like that seemed equivalent to a million.

"Would you like to meet him? We're getting together at the park just about now." And so we walked over to

Washington Square Park, and in a few minutes, a tall, handsome guy came strolling towards us, with two huge beautiful Borzoi hounds on a long leash bounding ahead of him. What style, what grace, what *chutzpah!* At that point I thought, well, if anyone can pull it off, it may well be this fellow. Those hounds did it. And so I was introduced to Stanley Kubrick. We talked for a few moments, then he and Howard were gone, the last time I saw either of them.

The film, incidentally, did get made; it was Kubrick's second, and flopped as the anti-war movie he intended it to be. But in its second incarnation, it was picked up by an impresario of the lurid named Joseph Levine, owner of the Rialto movie house, which showed soft porn and sensational films slightly off Broadway. There it made some money as the re-titled *Fear and Desire* by displaying posters of half-clad women victims of the film's violence.

Still, it was a beginning of the social conscience Kubrick displayed in his great films, *Dr. Strangelove, A Clockwork Orange*, and *Paths of Glory* (in my opinion the greatest anti-war protest of all). One can forgive him *Eyes Wide Shut*, a remake of a turn-of-the-century Schnitzler play that was completely out of synch with our times—perhaps, towards the end, Kubrick had spent too much time living in England (as had Sackler, who died too young there). But he did also make *Barry Lyndon* (another historical film, set in the eighteenth century) that the Harvard philosopher and film buff Stanley Cavell called the best film ever made—which I doubt, but it certainly is one of the most beautiful.

Grace Paley

The obvious thing about Grace Paley's work and life is her radical intervention in the stream of American literature of the mid- and late twentieth century. Radical in language, subjects, politics, she came on like an original blast of fresh air at the end of the formalist fifties, the almost entirely male-dominated literature of the fifties. I remember the pleasure well, the rapture even, of that voice when her short stories began appearing. There were the rhythms of New York speech, inflected with the Jewish rhythms and intonations of her upbringing and surroundings, alive with its snap, crackle, pop—a bit of Odets, some of Bellow, an antici-pation of Philip Roth even, some Edna Millay and Emma Goldman in her sexual freedoms, but wholly original, her own, always a woman's voice, with its concerns about Papa, Mama, aunts; about the playgrounds of Brooklyn and the Village and the young mothers of different races, united in the haze of their glory and confusion about what comes next, the outrage that fueled their feminist politics and left positions. All of that was Grace.

The first time I saw her I thought she was a bag woman the way she dressed, unconcerned about the niceties and expectations, though at a Feminist Press event in later years I sat next to her and saw that she could manage a more conventional appearance. But that first image remains as a badge of honor in my book. It coexists with the first time I saw Dorothy Day in the home of Allen Tate and Caroline Gordon around 1952 in Minneapolis. The Tates wanted Dorothy Day to talk about her religion (Allen Tate had recently converted to Catholicism), but she insisted on talking about the grave diggers' strike then in progress in New York. She and her paper, *The Catholic Worker*, had taken the side courageously, as usual, of the strikers against the Cardinal. She too dressed like a bag lady; she too spoke New York. She and Grace Paley occupy my private pantheon of sisterhood and sainthood.

Isaac Rosenfeld

Isaac died tragically young and alone at age thirty-eight, of a heart attack, in a room in Chicago. Wallace Markfield's novel *To an Early Grave*, later the film *Bye, Bye, Braverman*, was inspired by Isaac Rosenfeld's death. The death occurred after he left a two-year teaching stint in the Humanities Program of the University of Minnesota, where I met and knew him, not too well, but well enough to be influenced decisively by him. I had read an essay of his about a year earlier, on East European writing, in *Partisan Review*, when a phrase caught my attention. The phrase was about something totally useless, which he said "would help like cupping the dead." I didn't realize why it stuck in my mind until a few pages later. The phrase was a translation of a well-known Yiddish expression, *"Es vet helfn vi a toiten bankes,"* that I had known all my life, somewhere in the deep recesses of my being. Now this use of Yiddish in translation, or even in the original, is a commonplace, but then it hit me like a wonderful and surprising revelation. One could do that! There was a whole world lying under one's skin, a veritable Atlantis, for some of us who had grown up in first and second generation Yiddish-speaking and -reading communities, which we had put behind us in our quest for a place in the "real" America. Rosenfeld was among the first to include that kind of material and language in his work.

When Rosenfeld appeared at Minnesota and I met him for the first time, I told him about the impact that phrase in his piece had had on me. He was pleased and thoughtful and responded, in the honest and direct way characteristic of him, "You know, I did that at a certain point. As I think about it now, I used stuff in my writing from my Wilhelm Reich interest, from movies, from jazz, from popular culture generally, largely to liven up my English. Yiddish was my first language, and I always feel my English is somewhat flat, lacking an emotional dimension, that all that other material might provide." All this told to someone he had just met, and a mere teaching assistant at that.

His one novel, *Passage From Home*, might have "flat" parts, though the obligatory Passover seder scene in it is alive and powerful, as is the total effect of the book. His essays and stories were wonderful; all of us were swept away by one in which a guy is shaving and doesn't know when to stop, so shaves his whole body. A bit of Kafka, a bit of Freud (or Reich), but all of it Isaac—the smart one in the friendship with Bellow, according to Milton Mayer, speechwriter for Robert Hutchins at the University of Chicago, who knew them all and was a colleague of mine at Massachusetts for several years. The Bellow relationship was long-standing, Isaac being the subject of at least one Bellow story, and of the dedication of another, but their closeness may be best displayed in their Yiddish parody of "The Love Song of J. Alfred Prufrock," one of whose lines, *"Ich vehr alt, Ich ver alt, / Un mein pupik vert kalt"* ("I grow old, I grow old / and my belly button becomes cold"), deserves immortality.

Besides his giving me and my generation permission to use our Jewish past, what I liked about him was his common sense and irreverence. He could be wrong at times, as when he said to me after his first semester of teaching, "What a racket. Getting paid for reading and talking about books!" But he couldn't take too much of it, after all, and wanted to go back to just writing, even in isolation. I also used to usher him and his wife Vasiliki and their children in free at the Fine Arts movie house I managed for a few months near the campus. He always had a fine response, liking Chaplin in *Limelight*, for example, holding up two breakfast kippers while giving a suicidal Claire Bloom a speech on the importance of life.

Rosenfeld's most precious instruction for me occurred after a debate at the University Hillel where he skewered the rabbi in a discussion of the Book of Job. I invited him to our apartment for a drink; he came, and asked us what we were taking in this, our second graduate year. I said a seminar with Allen Tate on Critical Theory. He asked, "Does he have a kop?" I said, What? He repeated the question, and then I understood. Yiddish for did he have a head on his shoulders—was he smart? To even entertain such a question, such a sacrilegious thought in that New Critical era, never would have crossed my mind. "Now that you mention it, I don't really know. Every time we ask a question, he retreats to Greek." I do think Tate was smart, very smart, but the ability to entertain such skepticism about accepted "truths," the implicit injunction to think for one's self and follow your own truths was a lifelong gift. Thank you, Isaac.

Saul Bellow

For many years my favorite wine store was the Big Y on Routes 5/10 north of Northampton—once arguably the largest and best wine shop in the Northeast outside of New York. Entering it one afternoon, I stopped to talk with the clerk, who had been a grad student at UMass. He knew wines and was my *consigliere*. That day he opened the conversation by saying, "My mother would have liked to be here today." "Your mother? Why is that?" "Because she would have liked to see Saul Bellow. There he is, at the back of the store." And sure enough, there he was, mid-height, in a peaked cap like those worn on flight decks, and wearing a simple, tan, zippered windbreaker. He was standing in the expensive wine section, with three young people—former students of his, I soon learned, from the University of Chicago, paying him a visit in his Vermont summer home, not far north. Bellow came down here to buy wine, my friendly clerk informed me. I said to him, I never do this sort of thing, but I must go over to speak to Bellow.

And so I did. Polite and somewhat deferential, I introduced myself, and he was surprisingly open and friendly in return. I said he had published one of my wife's poems, "My Two Grandfathers," in an issue of *The Noble Savage*, a spirited literary journal he edited and published for four numbers in the sixties, and later wrote a blurb for her first book,

Between Wars & Other Poems. He pretended to remember her and I pretended to believe him. I went on to say we knew many people in common, mostly from our days at Minnesota—where I had arrived a year after Bellow left his teaching job in Humanities. Young though he was, and the author by then only of *Dangling Man* and *The Victim*—interesting works, but not books that would make him famous and a Nobel laureate—he was a legend around campus, people carrying short stories of his in their breast pockets, like holy talismans. So we talked of this one and that one, who had died, who had moved to California. Finally, I said that Anne and I were literary executors for Mary Doyle Curran, whose 1947 book, *The Parish and the Hill*, the Feminist Press had recently published and was keeping in print. "She adored you," I said, "Even though you called her 'Mary Cock-eyed Doyle'!" Mary wore very thick glasses. They had met at Yaddo, and for years there was a lively exchange of letters between them, including in some expressions of Mary's gratitude for an occasional unsolicited cash gift when she was strapped for money. Saul got a far-away look in his eye and replied, "Mary *RITA* Cock-eyed Doyle!"

From that moment, I too adored Saul Bellow, though for some time I couldn't read or teach his work because of the dour turn some of it took (*The Dean's December*, for example). In earlier times, he and Norman Mailer sat on my shoulders, guides through the shoals of American life and literature—to be replaced for the past two decades or more by Philip Roth, extraordinary chronicler of American life over fifty years. But Bellow is back for me, too. I'm not sure about Mailer, but Bellow will endure, having created several masterpieces. Among his shorter works, *Seize the Day* has received ample recognition and celebration, but "The Old System," less known, I would place in the company of Joyce's "The Dead," and Tolstoy's *The Death of Ivan Ilyich*. Among his novels, *The Victim* is worth many readings in its complex take on anti-Semitism and related human misreadings of reality. As is *Mr. Sammler's Planet*, which I avoided for years because of its traces of ugly and primitive racism, but upon rereading found full of wisdom, about family, about survival, about no choice but living on this planet, no alternative world available. That is a theme throughout Bellow's work—the here and now, no transcendence up or down. *Herzog* is still my favorite. Neurotic, self-pitying creep (as some critics have described him) though the central character may be, he is Bellow's traveler through a secular *Divine Comedy*, vouchsafed at the end as he lies in his hammock in the Berkshires, regarding his place in the universe, with a vision of redemptive peace and love.

I even forgive him his last work, *Ravelstein*, in his affection for the Allan Bloom-like "hero," that intellectual fop. Because in the story, when the guy befouls his vastly expensive sport coat, just bought in Paris with earnings from a book like *The Closing of the American Mind*, it doesn't matter. What matters is the intellectual seriousness, and the commitment to life, to a full life carried to its extreme, whether intellectually, sexually, or even crazily. The second half of the book is autobiographical, about Bellow's near-fatal illness shortly before, and one then realizes it is all a meditation on death (the fop has died)—which means, how should one live one's life? The answer to that lies at the heart of all Bellow's work: seriously but not somberly, in the here and now; this is what we have.

Want, want, want—that's okay, it is the human condition. Seize the day.

An aside on James Atlas's big and authoritative biography of Bellow: He gives us where Bellow was, where and when, how much money he had or didn't have, where and when, his attachments, romantic and professional. He ascribes Bellow's position in his family, among strong brothers and father, as the clue to the dynamics of his work. All useful facts and conjectures, but about his love life and marriages, Bellow told a mutual friend of ours and his, who repeated it to me, "This biographer was my Kenneth Starr."

Mary Rita and I salute you, *il miglior fabbro* (Eliot's dedication of *The Waste Land* to Pound, echoing Dante's dedication of *The Divine Comedy* to an earlier master: "The better maker.")

John Berryman:
The Imaginary Jew

What are you reading?" That was the first thing I remember Berryman saying to me as he sat down at my table in the coffee shop—The Dutch Treat—that we all went to in Dinkytown, near the English Department offices at the University of Minnesota. I had met him and attended his lecture on *The Tempest*, the most brilliant I had heard then or since, at the recommendation of a friend, an artist, who took his class and had photographed him. He was then an assistant professor in Humanities. The English Department did not accept him, or Bellow, or Rosenfeld—writers, not scholars— until years later. I answered, *"Partisan Review*; a story called 'The Machiavellians' by Saul Bellow, who used to teach here, too. The first chapter of a novel called *The Adventures of Augie March*." "What do you think of it?" "If he can keep it up in this way, it will be the best book of the century!" "Oh, Saul." "What do you mean, Oh, Saul?" "He's very good, very smart, and I rather like what he's doing in this book, the language— we were at Princeton together." No one is a hero to his valet (or friend), though I was wrong about that—he and Bellow were, indeed, always close, Bellow writing a beautiful introduction and tribute to Berryman's posthumous unfinished novel, *Recovery*, about his recurrent struggles with alcoholism.

"Have you read his earlier books, *Dangling Man* and *The Victim*?" I hadn't, and he urged me to read them and then we'd meet and talk. Two weeks later we sat together again and he asked me what I thought of them. "Wonderful, though the first one, *Dangling Man*, made me think, it was slow; *The Victim* blew me away, it's fantastic in every way!" He stared at me for a moment and said emphatically, "No, it's too neurotic. It goes around and around, never really settling anything. If the editorial board of *Partisan Review* could write a collective novel, that would be it." When I got to know several of those members of the editorial board years later, I had to honor Berryman's perspicacity, one more time.

He really was brilliant, learned, tortured, of course, as is well known. When I knew him he was sober, trying hard to live the AA regimen, day to day, as he said, and succeeding. Later came *The Dream Songs*, renown, the Pulitzer Prize, much anguish, and suicide. I honor him for his work and call him the Imaginary Jew, the title of his prize story in *Kenyon Review* in 1945. Here is the penultimate page of his novel, among the Author's Notes:

I. In my old story ["The Imaginary Jew"], a confrontation as Jew is resisted, fought, failed—at last given into symbolically. I identified at least with the persecution. So the 'desire' (was it?) is at least 25 years old.

II. PLUS after that, *The Black Book* [three poems in it a verse sequence about the Jews under Hitler]—abandoned—obsessed—perhaps now take it up again? *My position is certain.*

III. Horror of anti-Semitism.
      Excitement over Babel! Buber! The Hasidim! Bloch's
      music! Pascal's *Hebraism* in 'conversion'! WCW's
            [William Carlos Williams] Jewish blood!
      love for S., first doctor I ever felt *anything* for.
      resentment of Cal's [Robert Lowell] tiny Jewish blood,
            Daiches' *full* heritage.
      flourishing of Freud and Einstein.
      Jewish girls.
      Yiddish songs and slang.
      my Hebrew effort. Peret and Bargebecher(?).
      regular Old Testament study at last, this year.
      my anthology of Yiddish poetry! (till lately—why
            kept?)
      unique devotion to *Job*—texts, study, translation
            begun.
      resented/liked name 'Berryman' *being thought Jewish.*

William Phillips

After William's death his wife Edith Kurzweil, editor
for a short time of *Partisan Review* (*PR*), asked me
to contribute something to a 2003 memorial issue of *PR*.
I wrote a three-page tribute to William, a respectful piece
about the liberating impression he made upon me and of
our work together on the Coordinating Council of Literary
Magazines (CCLM) from 1967 to '72. I opened that essay
with the following paragraph:

> I first met William Phillips in 1952 or '53 at the University
> of Minnesota, when I was a T.A. in English and he was a
> visiting professor for a year in the Humanities Program. It
> was a heady time, with Isaac Rosenfeld and John Berryman
> also *in situ*, along with Phillips among the smartest and
> most interesting people I had met in academe. William cut
> a romantic and somewhat raffish figure for me, in his blue
> work shirts and, when he wore them, thick, loosely-knot-
> ted woolen ties (unlike the button-down rep tie that was
> then *de rigueur* in English Departments). Of course I was
> in awe of him as editor of the journal I read avidly as an
> undergraduate in New York in the post-war forties. When
> he spoke to me, I hung on every word, often interrupted
> by laughter (he could be very funny).

I then went on to discuss in some detail the history of

CCLM, from its origins in 1961 at a meeting of twenty-five editors of various journals meeting in St. Paul, Minnesota, that created the Association of Literary Magazines of America, CCLM's forerunner, to my leaving the organization in 1972. I concluded the piece with the following:

> William continued to try to hold the organization together for many years, as it grew in budget and numbers. But finally he had to leave CCLM to its own destiny. CCLM and its successor have continued to struggle to achieve some of the goals we had originally, and somewhat successfully, set for ourselves and the community of literary journals. William Phillips's contributions to the American literary community were unparalleled and central, as they were to many of the deeper issues of our collective intellectual life.

All of the above remains true, but of course there is more to add.

During that CCLM time I remember taking a long walk with William from his house on West 12th Street through the Village, with him in a reflective mood. He pointed out houses and apartments where people he had known, many celebrated in the academic and literary world from the thirties on (when *PR* began), had lived. "There's where Margaret Mead lived," he said, for example, and shortly thereafter, "I knew a lot of crazy people here." And it came to me then that he was certainly not crazy. Neurotic probably, nervous, obsessive, manipulative, thin-skinned, quick to take offense or sense an enmity or hostility—but not a Delmore Schwartz by any means. All of his "symptoms and characteristics" came out of a long, engaged life "making it" in New York, that toughest arena.

He was an excellent editor, from whom I learned a lot, seeing him cut through to the heart of a piece of writing or argument, and watching him run meetings. On that walk he said he was looking for a new managing editor and I was able to recommend Mary (Mel) Heath, our cherished managing editor—and later co-editor—at *The Massachusetts Review*, who wanted for personal reasons to leave Amherst. She was hired, spent a most interesting year at *PR*, which was then coming out of Rutgers. She was part of an entourage, mostly of women, who, in her words, took care of William—he was an attractive man, after all, and a sympathetic one, cosmopolitan charm combined with down-to-earth direct-ness. She wasn't there for the imbroglio with Rutgers about who owned the journal, when the university, among other things, challenged William's spending on literary lunches and dinners. It wasn't all that much, about $1500 over the year, I heard, which William thought a right and a necessity for the literary high culture. After all, he once explained to me, business spent vastly more than that on their notorious expense accounts, and what was more important for the life of American culture? Who could argue with him? Especially when I did enjoy some fine meals and wine in New York.

Rutgers padlocked the offices of *PR*, but William prevailed, after a court battle, leaving Rutgers for Boston University with the journal, and a professorship, firmly in his possession for several more years. It was a victory, but also presaged a defeat. After his death, John Silber, the hard-nosed President of B.U., ended support of the journal, forcing it to close down. Thus the end of an era—in its last days more conservative than in its glory days shortly after World War II. At that time, it brought the European intellectual world to us—Sartre, Camus, Orwell, Raymond Aron, the anti-Communist left intellectuals, et al.—which our generation hungrily awaited and devoured in *PR* issue by issue. In its last decades it had already become less read and less relevant. There is something of a cautionary tale in William's tenaciously holding on for a lifetime to an enterprise whose time, in a sense, had run out.

Harold Brodkey &
Erica Jong

In a novel called *The Return of Philip Latinovich*, by a renowned Yugoslav writer who lived down the street from us the year I was a Fulbright professor in Zagreb, the writer-hero of the story returns towards the end of his long life to the village he had come from. Sitting in the local café day after day listening to the conversations going on around him, he reflects that not once did any of them concern literature or literary matters, which had been central and all-consuming interests in his life. He is cast into deep doubt, an existential crisis, about how he had chosen to dedicate his life! I have thought often about this story and its gloomy truth.

Except for students, other academics, or literary professionals, I never encounter anyone in coffee shops, bars, trains, on vacations, reading and discussing really "serious" literature. Also in my experience, most writers tend to talk, when with other writers, about agents, publishers, royalties.

Until in an elevator in an apartment building on 86th Street and Broadway in Manhattan, I stood next to a man engrossed in a quality paperback copy of a novel by Tobias Smollet, that eighteenth-century stalwart, known, for all practical purposes, only to literary insiders. Unable to restrain myself, I asked the reader if he was a teacher, or, less likely, a student. "No," he replied off-handedly, "I'm just reading it for pleasure." Then he got off the elevator and I radiated with wonder. At last!

I related this incident to my friend in the building, a high school remedial reading teacher, in whose apartment Anne and I were staying for a couple of days. "Oh," she said, "that must have been Harold." Harold who?

"Harold Brodkey," she replied, "He lives upstairs. Would you like us to invite him for dinner?" Yes, of course, and we did indeed have dinner with him, who was then at the height of his career, with a stunning long story in *The New Yorker*. There went my radiant wonder. I still await an ordinary non-literary reader of Smollet.

I met Harold one more time.

In our never-ending quest for support in getting funding for CCLM, William Phillips had induced George Plimpton, then still editor of *Paris Review*, I believe, to throw a party for us at his Sutton Place apartment. William and Plimpton had been co-chairs of the "New York Intellectuals for Robert Kennedy" during the ill-fated 1968 year, and had continued their relationship. I enjoyed the photographs of Plimpton in the ring with Archie Moore, or quarterbacking for the Detroit Lions (one play). Among the literary lions in attendance were Norman Mailer, Manuel Puig, Gordon Lish (the egotistic fiction editor), and Harold Brodkey, accompanied by his tall, blonde male lover. As I talked with Brodkey, Erica Jong walked in and approached us. She had spent the night at our house in Amherst when she had come to do a reading, shortly after *Fear of Flying* appeared, but just before it took off as an iconic best-seller. I had liked her in her then uncertainty about the book's future and her personable, no-side, manner. Jerry Liebling got a good picture of her at that time. So I was quick to introduce her to Brodkey. What I blurted out was, "Erica, I'd like you to meet the best writer in New York, Harold Brodkey!" What a fatal speech to offer two hungry literary lions! Eager to make amends, I blurted out, again, with a red face, "I mean, the second best writer in New York." I still cringe with embarrassment when I remember that—and she had inscribed our copy of *Fear of Flying* "For Anne and Jules, With affection, Erica."

Brodkey died a short while later, of AIDS, and I never saw Erica again, except on TV. I continue to admire her and her work—and feel contrite. My son Robert, an undergraduate at Columbia at the time, accompanied me to that party and was a witness to all this, which he never fails to remind me of.

Irving Howe

In 1977 I sent Irving Howe a copy of my recently published book on Abraham Cahan, *From the Ghetto: The
Fiction of Abraham Cahan*, a work that I had begun in 1970–
71 by reading Cahan's five-volume memoir, in Yiddish, in a
small office at the Kennedy Institute in Berlin. He acknowl-
edged receipt, thanking me for my "little book." Since he and
Kenneth Libo had just come out with that indispensable *big*
book, *World of Our Fathers* (over seven hundred pages), he
was perfectly right to call my book "little" (only 161 pages).
Still, Irving, "A small book, but mine own." You could have
been more generous. I felt the put-down, just as I felt something similar previously towards the writer Harvey Swados
at his memorial service in Manhattan, when Howe spoke of
Harvey's career. I had always admired Swados, and he had
been a colleague at the University of Massachusetts, along with
Chinua Achebe, who had come to the memorial service with
me. In his youth Swados had belonged to the same group of
Shachmanites (liberal Trotskyites) that Howe had, so I was
rather surprised by what I thought was a somewhat conde-
scending tone towards Swados's work. Was it that Harvey
had "stood fast," still writing about the hardship of life for
workers "on the line?"

That was a side of Irving Howe at various points in
his career, somewhat tone deaf or imperious towards the

Other—whether denouncing the tactics of the young rebels
of the sixties; lecturing Ralph Ellison on what black writers
should write; or, most notoriously, declaring Jewish American
Literature dead because with the end of immigration it had
lost its basis. He has been often called to task for all of that,
and he certainly grew out of his narrow view of our Jewish
American Literature, becoming for most of his late years the
distinguished head of the Judaic Studies Program at CUNY
Graduate Center. Howe worked and developed steadily; his
writing improved, I believe, from bang-bang to an enviable
richness of tone and pace, and became a supreme instrument
for his serious thought and reflection. Our relationship, too,
grew, improving markedly after 1982. I was on sabbatical
in New York, working at the Columbia University Library
on an essay on Jewish ethnicity for a special issue on Jews
for Stanley Diamond's *Dialectical Anthropology* journal. I am
sure of the year, because that was when the disastrous Israeli
invasion of Lebanon occurred, culminating in the horrendous
massacre of Palestinians in two refugee camps, Shantilah
and Sabra. The news of that made me sick, heartsore, and I
wandered down Broadway in a daze, finally calling Diamond
to say that I could not write that piece now. He talked me
around, and I did eventually do it. It was one of only two
essays in the issue not anti-Israel; the other was by Harold
Bloom. But since that awful Lebanese War, I have fasted on
Yom Kippur (I had abandoned the practice two years after
my Bar Mitzvah) so as not to forget that Israel was complicit
in the evil.

Shortly after the facts became known, Irving Howe had

a letter in the *New York Times* condemning that action and criticizing Israel for its part in it. The letter surprised and heartened me. I called Howe to thank him for coming out as he had. His response was so unlike the earlier Howe I knew! He said, in a humble (yes!) voice, "Oh, thank you, Jules. My friends here in New York are angry with me for going public like that." I told him that, on the contrary, he spoke for and expressed the feelings of many of us American Jewish intellectuals and academics. As indeed he did, and I like to think he was heartened by my call, as I had been by his letter.

Two years later he accepted my invitation to be the keynote speaker at an Institute for Advanced Study in Humanities (which I directed at UMass Amherst) conference on Orwell's 1984 to be held at the Kennedy Memorial Library in Boston. He came; his talk was wonderful; it was a sparkling occasion. He was at the top of his form.

A few years later, I saw him for the last time, at a restaurant across from Lincoln Center. He had been ill, had aged, but his greeting was warm, and he introduced me around the table to his wife and friends. Later that night, after the opera, I recalled the very first time I met Howe—in Cambridge, in 1957, where he gave an informal talk at a gathering for *Dissent*. He had recently returned from Greece, his first wife's homeland—his first trip there, perhaps his first to Europe itself. I was certainly no sophisticate myself, my first trip abroad five years away, but I was struck by the "gee-whiz" aspect of his response to that wider world. It came to me then that he was just another New York kid growing up and out of the Depression, aspiring to and ultimately arriving at that other world more attractive: literature, high culture, high ideals, as so many others had and would. He had left the streets, and his father running after him calling "Oiving, Oiving, come home!" Steadily growing, steadily at his last—I love the title of one of his books, *Steady Work* (from a Chelm tale about waiting for the Messiah); he did come home, after a long and honorable life's work, enriched and enriching. We'll not see his like again.

Cynthia Ozick

At William Phillips's memorial service at the Ethical Culture Society, Cynthia Ozick gave a fine talk, straight from the shoulder, no false sentimentality or bonhomie. Someone had spoken of the charismatic Susan Sontag, who had wowed the group around *Partisan Review* when she appeared on the scene. I had squired Ms. Sontag around our campus for two days when she gave the opening talk for my Institute, to an overflow house, and she wowed me, and I found her surprisingly warm, funny, straight-talking, capable of humility, too. Anyway, Cynthia, from behind her owlish glasses and severe demeanor, said she had not been to those parties with Lionel Trilling and the other luminaries. She was not as beautiful as Sontag (who was?), simply a hard-working, serious graduate student at Columbia, humbly aspiring to a place, maybe, in the Republic of Letters. She had read her way out of her father's pharmacy in the Bronx and dared beyond all expectations to have a literary career. Which she has achieved nobly, to the enrichment of us all.

What she didn't recount at that ceremony was an incident she described that occurred in her class with Trilling that she wrote about in a *Forward* piece (May 7, 1999). She recalled raising her hand and suggesting that Marx, Freud and Einstein being Jewish might "signify something." Trilling "blew up at me, was enraged, outraged.... I had sullied—

"vulgarized" is closer to the response—his class.... I was made to feel SHAME, shame over having introduced the idea of Jewishness as a contributing force." She says it was not much of an anecdote, though I would disagree—it is a most telling episode, capturing some of that 1950s zeitgeist. What I experienced at Minnesota in those years was similar, though a few people, the New York crowd and their allies in the Humanities Program, refreshed and surprised me by their rich repertoire of Jewish jokes at their parties. I sensed something subterranean, and liberating from genteel English Department shackles, was going on.

Cynthia freed herself early, which enabled her to tap into the rich vein of Jewishness. I have not always agreed with her views or liked all of her work—though her 2004 novel, *Heir to the Glimmering World*, one of her more recent, is a wonderful book, with a fresh slant on the refugee-in-New-York tale and much else, told with her impeccable style. When she first burst on the scene with "Envy: Or, Yiddish in America," it was easy to recognize it as the best story ever about the world of the Yiddish writers in New York left without an audience, a reading public, after World War II (who claimed they only needed good translators, like that inferior writer, Isaac Bashevis Singer, to show how good they were)—and that its author was immensely gifted. When the narrator, a putative translator, tells these envious nags to get off her back, she has declared the independence of a new generation of Jewish American writers.

But not separate from the Jewish world, as she knew or imagined it. The title story of her first book, *The Pagan Rabbi and Other Stories*, is transgressive, wonderfully weird, deep with the knowledge, and dare one say it, love, of that world. Even in its weirdest aspects (which were taken to heart by Mark Mirsky and others indebted to her example), she has always had a wonderful position about fictional texts versus religious ones that encourages, if not the absolutely "weird," then demonic and crooked lanes. More on that aspect and the significance of her views about fiction later in this piece.

There were times in her early career when she took what I thought were crazy positions, though not in her fiction, opting for a Jewish English, for example, (a form of New Yiddish? Or what?), and advocated following the non-changing truths given to us from Mt. Zion. I argued with her once at an MLA panel we were on, taking the position that Jewish life and culture changed through history and would continue to change. Surely we would say now, with the increasing role and open voices of women in the rabbinate and Jewish affairs generally, we are in the midst of the most profound changes in Jewish life and learning in millennia. At the same time, she balanced those positions with good advice to us back-sliders: to blow through the narrow end of the shofar (our Jewishness), not to go for the big end, the "universal," where we would only blow out air.

Sometime in the seventies, I think, we met again at a Jewish conference at Columbia, on a wintry day. Her husband and I, and Norma Rosen's husband, good friends of Cynthia's, were wearing Russian type fur hats and went out for coffee together. Was that costuming just an odd coincidence, or a reflection of a new reality—a moment of turning, on many fronts, back to conscious *Yiddishkeit* or Judaic bonding? There had been the Six-Day War, the Yom Kippur War of 1973, and the Ethnic Revival, post-sixties. More and more Judaic Studies Programs were being formed, including one I was a part of at my university, demonstrating that we must assert *"Vir zenen doh"* ("We are here").

Norma Rosen has written novels, about the holocaust and other serious matters, that have been well received but deserve more attention, and a fine historical fiction based on John Dewey and Anzia Yezierska. She came to a birthday party Milly Marmur, my dearest old friend and sometime agent, gave for me, but I have not seen her since. Her son Jonathan Rosen has been literary editor of the *Forward* and more recently writes for *The New Yorker* and other important journals. He and his generation have learned from our generation, but gone further in certain ways. His novel *Joy Comes in the Morning* has a healthy dose of irreverence, and a female rabbi heroine. She is Reform, but extremely religious, very sexy and scabrous. She says "shit" a lot, and yells at a taxi driver who has cut her car off, "It's a funeral, asshole!" There is an old *zayde* in the story who says, "God can kiss my bony ass," and then he cries. Rosen, like many others of his generation want to have it both ways—and to show us it can be done.

To go back to the good position I said earlier Ozick took on the nature of fiction: In a 2001 symposium in the *Forward* on "What is a Jewish Book?" she squared off with Ruth Wisse, the first professor of Yiddish at Harvard. Professor Wisse contributed one of her usual Jeremiads: "Our present anxiety about Jewish literature derives not from a slump in contemporary Jewish writing but from the insufficiencies of American Jewish life. An ignorant Jewry inhibits even the knowledgeable Jewish writer.... Add indifference to the ignorance, and Jewishness becomes silly putty." I admire the liveliness of the prose, but have problems with its sense.

Ozick takes a more surprising position—surprising only in view of her reputation in some quarters as a conservative and Jewish enforcer. "A Jewish book," she wrote, "is liturgy, ethics, philosophy, ontology.... A Jewish book is didactic. It is dedicated to the promotion of virtue attained through study.... To be a Jew is to be a good citizen, to be responsible, to be charitable, to respond to society's needs." But, she goes on, "To be a novelist is the opposite—to seize unrestraint and freedom, even demonic freedom, imagination with its reins cut loose.... What we want from novels is not what we want from the transcendent liturgies of the synagogue. The light a genuine novel gives out is struck off by the nightmare calculations of art: story, language (language especially), irony, comedy, the crooked lanes of desire and deceit." What a great statement! Of course she doesn't always achieve that—which writer has? Even her hero Henry James—but she comes close, more often than not. *Bis a hundert un tvantsig, liebe schvester!* May you go on until 120, dear sister Cynthia!

Leslie Fiedler

My first job interview in the academy occurred in 1954, when I attended my first MLA meeting, shortly after passing my doctoral examinations. I was testing the market, as they say. William Van O'Connor, one of my advisers, introduced me to Leslie Fiedler, then head of the English Department at the University of Montana. He immediately left us alone, the Chairman and I facing each other in a big empty hallway. Fiedler's first remark made an indelible impression: "I can't hire any more Jews." Did I hear correctly? "We already have Seymour Betsky [and he named another landsman whose name I have forgotten] and myself. Chametzky, Betsky and Fiedler, it sounds like an East Side clothing store." In spite of myself, I smiled. "The American Legion is already picketing us as being a bunch of radical New Yorkers." (Fiedler was actually from New Jersey.) Senator McCarthy had only recently been rebuffed in the Army hearings, but the fears lingered on.

Despite that inauspicious beginning, our relationship grew very companionably in the years to come. I admired Fiedler's work enormously for its original insights and daring. English departments, especially the American divisions, made fun of his "Come Back to the Raft, Huck Honey" essay, and his identifying the interracial, homoerotic strain in much of classic American texts and popular culture (Ishmael and Queequeg, Natty Bumpo and Chingachgook, Huck and Jim, The Lone Ranger and Tonto). In time they had to choke it down, eat their words, agree to his prescience and influence (as Fiedler had that of D.H. Lawrence's pioneering work along similar lines in the twenties). *"Tempus fugit, un mir nudget,"* as my Hebrew teacher used to say. "Time passes, and we continue to nag."

Our personal rapprochement occurred in Berlin in 1970–71. Fiedler had come to lecture at the Amerika Haus and the Kennedy Institute (where I was a guest professor for that year). Werner Sollors, with whom I had become close, and I accompanied Leslie to the Director's office, where we all chatted amiably for a few minutes. We remarked on the barricades outside the building. The Director said, yes, we have to protect ourselves against demonstrations from the then-active groups of anti-American German radicals. "We even have police dogs in the basement in case they invade the building." Our response was instantaneous and horrified. Leslie gave our feelings immediate voice: "I can't lecture while being protected by police dogs! I am leaving at once." And he did, and we did. I think that was when any negative feelings I had about Fiedler melted away. Despite his salutary literary work, I resented his insensitive essay in the fifties about the Rosenbergs after their execution. Because of their letters from prison he seemed to justify their—to me and many others—excessive and brutal punishment. In those letters, he suggested, they had forfeited their humanity and our sympathy because of their inauthentic and, not to put too fine a point on it, Stalinist language. It was unworthy of him or anyone to make such a judgment, and I believe he ultimately regretted it. That episode in the Amerika Haus restored my good opinion of him.

The day before he had lectured in a room at the Kennedy Institute, where I introduced him. The students smiled (or smirked) to themselves as we stood in front of them: two somewhat portly middle-aging Jews, about the same medium height, both sporting fine Trotskyite goatees. Besides which, Leslie had been preceded by a poster showing him looking fierce and, yes, demonic or diabolic. The tufts of wild hair, looking almost like the proverbial horns we Jews were supposed to have, must have touched some residual chord in those students. It was a brilliant and fierce lecture, stunning them into unusual silence. No questions or comments from the audience.

The evening of our exit from the Amerika Haus, we met my wife and Werner's at a Greek restaurant that stayed open all night. Leslie's wife was also present. The previous night she had unexpectedly appeared, to Leslie's surprise, at his hotel when I walked him home. I wondered if she had come in order to catch him in flagrante delicto, but, alas, she only caught me. No matter. She was charming, intelligent, and good company. At the four-hour dinner, with lots of ouzo, she made wonderful and acute observations, and when Leslie spoke, he usually looked sideways at her—for her approval? I often wondered how much he owed her for his brave and original ideas. After having many children together, they ultimately divorced, she going off to Mexico to study with Ivan Ilich, he remarrying.

He was in a less challenging relationship, I was told by Irving Saner, who also lived in Buffalo, and who was one of those old-time book salesmen who used to circulate in the academy, spreading news and gossip as part of their welcome.

It was also a less productive, but, I was told, a bland and happier time for Leslie.

The night Mrs. Fiedler had been waiting at his hotel without his knowing she had come, I had spent walking and talking at length with Leslie, exchanging secrets, as it were. I told him of my closeness, for a short time, years earlier with the American Communist Party, though refusing to be recruited, finally breaking entirely with all that after reading, as a student, Orwell and various Trotskyite critiques. That was several years before Stalin's death and Khrushchev's revelations of Stalin's crimes. He reciprocated, telling me (and I hope I am not betraying a family secret), that his brother, who worked for the State Department, had told him years before that he would have nothing to do with him ever again. Because he was a radical Leslie should from then on not claim any relationship to him, which the brother would deny if confronted with it. And Fiedler was never more than a mild, unaffiliated Trotskyite, so far as I know. I also felt that he was deeply wounded by that rejection.

He was a great storyteller. At a Denver MLA meeting in the late seventies, he told me about meeting his friend Saul Bellow after Bellow had won the Nobel Prize in 1976. He asked Bellow what sort of difference the award had made in his life. Bellow replied that the main thing was that now many of his friends were asking him for money. After laughing at this, they talked on. When he was going to leave, Fiedler felt for his wallet. "Oh my god, Saul, I left my wallet in my hotel room. Could you lend me twenty for the cab?"

Tillie Olsen

Leo Marx brought Tillie to Amherst College for a year's visiting lectureship in 1969, where she precipitated a revolution whose effects are felt to this day. A grandmother in mini-skirts, she had already published a decade earlier the incomparable *Tell Me a Riddle*. Much has been written about that pioneering and deeply influential work, especially its title story. Less has been written about "I Stand Here Ironing," the monologue that opens the book. It became a mantra for the emerging feminist movement with its iconic image of an Ur-mother wielding an iron instead of the patriarchal knife of Abraham, explaining and justifying her life, importuning her daughter to free herself from the ancient victimhood of women. It is no exaggeration to say Tillie Olsen kicked off in her year there the feminist movement in the Pioneer Valley, home to five institutions of higher learning.

She was capable of three-hour lectures—especially on the plenitude of writers and works she introduced in a course she offered called "Broadening the Canon." I brought her reading list as the basis for the course of that name I gave in Berlin the next year, 1970–71, when I was invited as a guest professor to the Kennedy Institute for North American Studies of the Free University. The young woman assistant professor whom I asked to give a lecture on women in literature, Beate

Schopp-Schilling, went on to become the arbiter of women's issues in the Bonn government. The other assistant I asked to talk, on black writers, was Werner Sollors, whose dissertation director I became a few years later. Werner has been for several years Director of the Graduate Program in American Civilization at Harvard. His 1986 book, *Beyond Ethnicity*, is the most frequently cited and influential work in the field. So the ripple effect, the radiation, of Tillie Olsen's influence goes on and on.

At dinners with her cousin and my colleague Arlyn Diamond, she could be highly entertaining, lively, always "on" about feminism and related political matters. But she did have a kind of obsessive quality that I think slowed up her writing productivity. Of course in *Silences* she makes a strong case for the reasons slowing up or suppressing many women writers and putative writers—no rooms of their own, the pressures and traditional restraints upon women, forbidden education, little money of their own, the stereotyping of women's roles. She had experienced all of that, plus the stultifying working class jobs desperately needed to survive and raise a family during the Depression. Still, her painstaking scrupulousness in writing, the vast stores of references she accumulated in her minute handwriting on scraps of paper, illuminating, when put together, many dark or forgotten places in our literary past (as in her ground-breaking work on Rebecca Harding Davis's *Life in the Iron Mills*), did slow her up. My wife and another friend once spent an entire day with Tillie in Boston, searching for just the right 2H pencil she liked to use.

What Tillie Olsen did, what she accomplished, how her work still resonates, remains unique, and she is assured a place among the most important and influential writers of her generation.

Adrienne Rich, Anne Halley, Marilyn Hacker

I first met Adrienne Rich at a meeting of the New University Conference (NUC) at Wesleyan College in Connecticut, home of several ardent anti-Vietnam War academics. NUC had been organized, chiefly, I believe, by Paul Lauter and Florence Howe (then a married couple), and Louis Kampf and his then wife, Ellen Cantarow, as an anti-war outgrowth of the New Left. A collateral goal of the organization was to radicalize curriculum and teaching in colleges and universities. I had joined when we met in our living room in Amherst—my wife, Anne Halley, though actively anti-war, was not a joiner, except for the feminist encounter groups that sprang up shortly thereafter. So she did not meet Rich then, though deep into Adrienne's work. As a poetry editor of *The Massachusetts Review*, Anne corresponded and met with her, as I did, and published her poetry many times.

At Wesleyan Adrienne galvanized us with an outraged and painful reading of a poem by a male leading light of the time (Donald Hall? James Dickey?) in which was imagined the beating of a woman with a heavy belt and then her being tossed, or falling, from an airplane. Was it supposed to be funny? Or a fantasy of male supremacy? In any case it made us, mostly men there, keenly aware, for perhaps the first time, of the blithely accepted misogyny of our mainstream literature. It took a movement to change that.

So much grew out of the anti-war and civil rights movements, certainly feminism, and for many, as pluralism and minority presence grew to be the newly perceived reality about American identity, the Jewish connections. Sometimes, as in Adrienne's and Anne Halley's case, perhaps Denise Levertov's, as "half Jews." I remember Levertov's passionate anti-war speech at an Amherst rally, and years later divorced but joyous at a dinner party in Medford at the home of our mutual pacifist friends, Martin Green and Carol Hurd Green, encouraging Carol in her work on Dorothy Day and Ethel Rosenberg! Ethel Rosenberg. Carol, a Catholic, was an administrator and teacher at Boston College. She and Martin had two adopted African American children. That dinner party arose from The Movement.

Rich has recalled that her father, a Jewish doctor who grew up in the south, was totally assimilated, but that as she contemplated the Jewish part of her life, and of course the Holocaust, when in her early days she had thought of herself as neither Gentile (her mother was a Protestant southerner) nor Jew, and neither Yankee nor "rebel," she came to see that part of herself as more and more integral to her multi-faceted identity, and she embraced it. She goes into all these issues in her fine poem "Yom Kippur 1984" and in "Split at the Root: An Essay on Jewish Identity."

In the world in which she was raised, she writes in that extraordinary 1982 essay, "the world of acceptable folk was white, gentile (Christian, really), and had 'ideals,' (which

colored people and white 'common' people were not supposed to have). 'Ideals' and 'manners' included not hurting
someone's feelings by calling her or him a Negro or a Jew—
naming the hated identity." Rich goes on, "…writing this,
I feel dimly like a betrayer, of my father, who did not speak
the word; of my mother, who must have trained me in the
messages; of my caste and class; of my whiteness itself." It is
a brave essay, which she concludes as follows: "Sometimes I
feel I have seen too long from too many disconnected angles:
white, Jewish, anti-Semite, racist, anti-racist, once-married,
lesbian, middle-class, feminist, exmatriate southerner, split at
the root that I will never bring them whole.… This essay then
has no conclusions: it is another beginning for me. Not just a
way of saying, in 1982 Right Wing America, I too, will wear
the yellow star. It's a moving into accountability, enlarging
the range of accountability."

Thus Rich is the moral writer which that other doyenne
of fiction and criticism, Cynthia Ozick, might desire, though
they obviously don't share an ideology and a politics. Still,
Adrienne Rich is one of many who have taken the path of
"wearing the yellow star." What interests me is how other
women poets of roughly her generation, whom I have known,
have followed similar paths, emboldened and grateful to
Adrienne, though not necessarily going all the way with her,
through all her changes and dimensions, diving into every
wreck, all the myths of American life. But one can do worse.

When Anne Halley left for college, Wellesley, in
1945, her German physician mother told her, "You don't
have to tell people your father [also a doctor] is Jewish."

The parents had left Germany by 1936 with their young son, leaving Anne and her non-identical twin sister behind to be sheltered by an Aryan aunt for two years, before they could send for them in 1938. There perhaps was the latent source of her ardent feminism. The boy taken out, but not the girls? In one of her last essays (Anne died in 2004), in the 40th Anniversary Issue of *The Massachusetts Review* (1999–2000), she writes about the fate of a sensitive, wonderful Berlin Jewish editor, Edith Marcuse, sister of a prominent writer and later Stanford professor, Ludwig Marcuse, who got himself out, but left her behind to take care of their mother. Then she was murdered in Auschwitz. Not an unusual occurrence.

But back to Wellesley. She heeded the injunction to silence until there came a crucial event, minor in the grand scheme of things, but portentous. Her innocent sister had invited a nice boy from MIT to come to one of the freshmen mixers at the college. And he brought along some of his fellow frat members, from Sigma Alpha Mu, the Jewish fraternity. After the dancing, Anne overheard one of the Southern girls in the corridor telling another belle, "Well, I have known Jews before, but I never let one touch me." And that precipitated a crisis. Sheltered as a child in Nazi Germany, she had never heard an anti-Semitic remark outright, but there it was, here at Wellesley! After a long day turning it over in her mind, she moved into the corridor with its four Jewish girls at the other end of the tower hall, with whom she remained lifelong friends. And she was rarely if ever silent again about that invisible yellow star, writing often in condemnation of the barbaric turn of German life and the scent of ashes that was its legacy to the Jews. It was certainly not as bad here, by any stretch, but it was here, too. She never forgot. On her tombstone, in Hebrew, is engraved *"aishet chayil"* (Proverbs), "A virtuous woman" (or is it "valiant?") She was both.

Her early poems are often about the German Jewish, and half-Jewish (like Rich) identity, not recognized as truly Jewish by the Orthodox because of the patrilineal descent, but ironically entitled as a Jewish refugee from Nazism, as are all her children, born in the USA, to German citizenship if she chose to exercise that right (which she never did). On another front, her strong feminist poems in *The Bearded Mother*, make some people recoil, as does the title itself. Why? When she did a reading from the book in the feminist late seventies, to an academic audience, my colleague John Clayton, now writing Jewish stories and novels, came away ashen and said to me "How can you take it? It was like being kicked in the stomach." For him, who had been anti-war, but not present at Adrienne's reading of the poem about the beaten and killed woman, the felt kick was probably further down.

I have one more poet and a poem in mind. Some time ago, having recently returned from a month in Paris, where I spent two weeks in classes held in the Marais, I thought of Marilyn Hacker who resides half the year in Paris with her partner, a woman. Anne and I had met Hacker briefly in New York. Marilyn Hacker was among Anne's most admired contemporary poets and *MR* often published her poems. She had been married to a former UMass Amherst colleague, the far-out and wonderful black writer Sam Delany, another refusenik, like Hacker and Rich, to the dominance of the heterosexual mode. Hacker, too, is Jewish.

The poem that so resonates for me was also published in the 40th Anniversary Issue of *MR*:

Rue des Écouffes

The street is narrow, and it just extends
rue de Rivoli/rue des Rosiers
a street from which the children went away
clutching their mothers, looking for their friends,
on city buses used for other ends
one not-yet-humid morning in July.
Now kosher butchers co-exist with gay
boutiques, not gaily. Smooth-cheeked ephebes hold
    hands.
Small boys with forelocks trail after bearded men —
and I have dragged that story in again
and will inevitably next compare
the curtains of the creaky balcony
smelling of female exile, exhaled prayer
with the discreet shutters of the women's bar.

I like the way she backs off from the obvious: the Jewish survival after the war in that quarter, which had such a horrendous history of deportations, and the inevitable, almost obligatory, comparison of that, even if it is the old patriarchy, with the gay life there and the smell of "female exile." To her credit, she ironizes all of it. But it all gets mentioned and memorialized. Great.

Allen Ginsberg

One of the smartest co-editors of the *Norton Anthology*, John Felstiner, ends his lengthily astute introduction to Ginsberg and his place in Jewish American letters with quotes from Harold Bloom (negative: reading "Kaddish" is like being forced to "watch the hysteria of strangers"), and Saul Bellow (positive: "Under all the self-revealing candor is purity of heart"). John concedes that Ginsberg changed "the face of American poetry," but adds that the word for him is chutzpah. I go along with Bellow: candor, and heart. "Howl" was the great breakthrough work of our generation, and "Kaddish," for his mother who died in an insane asylum, his Jewish declaration of love for her, warts and all, and his heartbreak. When Ginsberg published "Howl" in 1953, I couldn't agree with his opening lines—I didn't see "the best minds of my [our] generation, destroyed by madness, starving hysterical naked,/dragging themselves through the negro streets at dawn looking for an angry fix," though undoubtedly there were some of those among Ginsberg's friends, but they were a fairly small, marginal and self-destructive bunch—I had seen some. There were many other "best minds" of different persuasions around, let's not exaggerate, but undoubtedly Ginsberg's raw and raunchy poem shattered the last vestiges of Eliot-esque, academic gentility and literary anemia. That was and has been of inestimable importance. Harold Bloom, as critic and teacher, did some of that important work, too, with his Freudianism, Romantic or Emersonian oracular style, interest in Kabbalah, so I cannot fathom his hostility to Ginsberg. In some crazy way, they are brothers under the skin, if Harold but let himself admit it.

For a long time I associated Ginsberg with the George McGovern (a good man who deserved better) disaster at the 1972 Democratic Convention in Miami Beach which I attended with my three sons, given tickets by an old friend from Minnesota who had been Hubert Humphrey's Press Secretary. Ginsberg didn't do much there, except sit in the mud in Flamingo Park with hundreds of other alternative life-style types, in trees, in tents, in a ripped T-shirt, rubbing his belly and intoning "Ummmm-ummmm." It was emblematic of all that went wrong with the organization and PR of that event, culminating in the nominee's acceptance speech at 2 a.m. Imamu Baraka was running around as well, that year wearing a Mao jacket, surrounded by thuggish Mau Mau-type body-guards, and there were some women in combat jackets and boots, all caught on television. Not good.

Over time, my impression of Ginsberg changed complete-ly. We did get him up to Amherst on March 22, 1986 (he inscribed the date for me in his *Collected Poems*), when he was wearing a three-piece flannel suit and was by then a professor at Brooklyn College. It was an historic occasion, for one thing because it was the only time he and James Baldwin met—a photograph of them together is the cover of an *MR* issue that deals with Ginsberg's 1965 Prague experience. That experience was the real reason for Ginsberg's appearance among us.

Andrew Lass, an anthropology professor at Mount Holyoke College, and in another part of his life a well-known Czech poet, had grown up in Prague with his American journalist parents and had been Ginsberg's cicerone and translator that year of 1965. On May 1, Ginsberg was crowned King of the May by the university students, an act of deviance that presaged the uprising of 1968 and the later Velvet Revolution. Andy had told me he thought he had a short film of the occasion. My excitement was predictable, and ultimately that was what brought the poet up—for he had never seen the footage either. We showed it to a full house in a local bookstore. Lass's film took less than 20 minutes, but it was gorgeous and fascinating—and the student rebellion in naming Ginsberg led to his expulsion by the regime. The secret police had also confiscated his journal, which was rather risqué, to say the least (and which we published in part in *MR*), and that became the ostensible cause of his ejection. He did eventually get the journal back, heavily censored. Ginsberg wrote all about it in the airplane taking him out of the country, in a poem called "Kral Majales," which ends as follows:

> And tho' I am the King of May, the Marxists have beat
> me upon the street, kept me up all night in the Police
> Station, followed me thru Springtime Prague, detained
> me in secret and deported me from our
> kingdom by airplane.

> Thus I have written this poem on a jet seat in mid
> Heaven.

Candor, and courage. Never mind chutzpah.

Finally, the part of Ginsberg I most respect. Not just his brave stands against war, nuclear weapons, environmental degradation and all that, but his extending friendship and support to all who needed it. One of my son Robert's best friends at Columbia College was writing a dissertation for a graduate degree on Lionel Trilling and Ginsberg—a connection between the two begun when Ginsberg was an undergraduate at Columbia and that others have commented on, including Ginsberg himself, and was hinted at in a Trilling story, "Of This Time, Of This Place"—which promised to be immensely illuminating about that relationship. This boy, Nat, a slight, good-looking Jewish kid from New Jersey, took a job teaching in New Orleans, and there he came out—a turn that surprised all his college friends, none of whom had realized earlier that he might be gay. Not too long afterwards, he was diagnosed with AIDS, which he endured bravely for some time. In his final sickness, his family refused to see him and so Robert left Chicago, where he was a graduate student, to spend a week with Nat at his bedside. During that bad period, Allen Ginsberg, in Colorado then, I believe, called Nat several times. He knew Nat only as someone who had corresponded with him about his own time at Columbia for the dissertation. Ginsberg's calls offered warm affection and regard—and were extraordinarily meaningful to Nat, as he told us when we visited him. Ginsberg, I've read, kept an elaborate, extensive file on all those in similar and other needy circumstances, frequently making helpful connections with and for them. Candor yes, courage yes, and most assuredly heart.

Kadya Molodowsky

Sometime during a summer in the sixties, Joseph Landis, editor then and through all these years of *Yiddish*, a precious journal out of Queens College in New York, invited me to speak at Camp Boiberek in Rhinebeck, New York. I had published an article on Abraham Cahan a few years earlier and he wanted me to talk about Cahan's Yiddish fiction. I had previously only heard of the camp and its funny name, and that it was dedicated to the use and perpetuation of the Yiddish language. Its summer denizens were supposed to study and speak the language all the time. A great cause, so I readily accepted. No fee, but very good old-time Jewish food, and the chance to meet Kadya Molodowsky, a legendary figure in the world of Yiddish poetry. She and her husband came there year after year.

Then quite advanced in age, they still edited their journal, *Surroundings*, published bimonthly from 1941 until 1974, out of their home on the Lower East Side. The journal was devoted to Yiddish poetry, with strict and careful attention to the correct usage, grammar, flavor of the language. Steadily smoking a cigarette, she accepted graciously the homage rendered her by person after person who knew her poems by heart and remembered them from childhood. There had been few poems in my childhood home, only Hebrew ones that I could read but not understand in the siddurs and other religious texts that were our only books. Though my parents spoke Yiddish almost all the time, I never knew about Yiddish poets until years later. I owe Kathryn Hellerstein, one of my co-editors on *Jewish American Literature: A Norton Anthology*, for much of that knowledge. Kathryn describes there in concise form all of Molodowsky's many works, in poetry, novels, plays, essays, as well as her life in Russia and Poland, until she came to America in 1935 already over forty, up to her death in 1975.

I am most grateful for her poem "God of Mercy," that I invariably teach in Jewish literature courses. Thirty-nine lines long, in four verses, here in Hellerstein's translation, in very small part, is the gist of it:

> O God of Mercy
> Choose—
> Another people.
> We are tired of death, tired of corpses We have no
>   more prayers.
> Choose—
> Another people.

It concludes:

> And O God of Mercy
> Grant us one more blessing—
> Take back the divine glory of our genius.

Very bitter, very sad, and how could it not be? Yet she was a delight in person, enjoying the summer camp, the people, the survival of the language, and in a quiet, dignified way, the homage.

Another gift of that two-day stay was meeting Shlomo Katz, then editor of *Midstream*, a monthly Zionist review, published by the Theodore Herzl Foundation. I wondered that he should be coming to a camp devoted to the perpetuation of Yiddish, which I thought Zionists had for years, in its early days, considered anathema, the language of the Diaspora Jews and of centuries of defeat and persecution. Well, that was too simple on my part, and Katz echoed my own view, that the language embodied a thousand years of Jewish history and could not be dismissed or forgotten. He enjoyed speaking and reading it, his first language. Like so many early Yiddishists and Zionists, who knew, wrote and read, and valued both languages. We got on very well, and he asked me to do a review for his journal, which I did, of Alfred Kazin's *Starting Out In the Thirties*. I regret not following up on that wonderful experience with more work for them, or never again visiting Boiberek. To mitigate my guilt, I have to say I did since then publish in *Yiddish* and have continued to be named on their editorial board, a point of pride for me. God of Mercy—and Justice.

Amos Oz, Shirley Kaufman, Abba Kovner

mos Oz came to the University of Massachusetts
Amherst campus at least twice in the 1980s. The Judaic
Studies Department had a breakfast with him before a talk,
and I arranged a luncheon the next day at the Institute for
a group of Jewish writers from the area to meet with him
for a more informal talk. He was friendly, open, a pleasure
to be with. I remember best his saying, in answer to one
question, I think Jay Neugeboren's, about the difficulties
with the Hebrew language for new people wanting to come
to Israel, especially writers, that it was a problem. The language changed so quickly, yet there was such a base for it,
going back to biblical Hebrew, and embodying as well the
experiences of various generations of Sabras (he was one)
and others coming in to the Land at various stages, that
newcomers always had a problem catching on or catching
up. But he welcomed us all, and extended an invitation
to me personally, afterwards, to come visit him in Israel.
Unfortunately I have never taken him up on that. I was
most tempted after reading *A Tale of Love and Darkness*, a
masterpiece, a beautiful, moving account of the Israel of
his childhood and young manhood, and especially of his
parents and their divergent backgrounds. Oz in that book

is an Israeli Tonio Kroeger, caught between the scholarly father's family history and the artistic mother and hers. Her suicide when he was a young man is the wrenching emotional heart of the book.

The language question came up with Shirley Kaufman, who had become a friend when she was a visiting poet for a semester in our department and lived down the street from us. She had done a very brave thing in her life, leaving a marriage to a successful physician in the Bay area and two grown daughters after falling in love with an Israeli scholar who was on a visiting professorship at the University of California in Berkeley. She married him, Hillel Daleski, a D. H. Lawrence expert, tall, handsome, substantial, ultimately a dean at the Hebrew University, and moved in 1973 permanently to Israel. She continued to write wonderful poems, and to love her new life, despite its ambiguities and difficulties.

On one of her visits back to the United States, I saw her again as the translator and interpreter for Abba Kovner, one of the most honored of Israeli poets, when they gave a joint reading at the Israeli Consulate in Boston. I told her what Oz had said about the language difficulties for newcomers, wondering what she thought about that. She quickly agreed. She said she had trouble with the rapid and complex Hebrew that Daleski and his friends were wont to get into. But she was improving all the time, and read well enough to be an excellent translator for Kovner's work; and her writing in English certainly didn't suffer. In fact, shifting between languages seems to have sharpened

her perception and use of each. Here's the beginning of
her poem called "Stones," from the eighties, that I like:

> When you live in Jerusalem you begin To feel the
> weight of stones.
> You begin to know the word Was made stone, not
> flesh.

Was it stone soup, after all, given to us Jews? That bitter
thought occurred to me years ago when we visited Sfad and
peered out at the rocky, lunar landscape that good Rabbi Isaac
Luria saw from the window of his stone cell at the end of the
sixteenth century. He then invented the modern Kabbalah
that said, in effect, this readily observable world couldn't be
the real one. Who could blame him, his family having been
expelled by Spain a hundred years previously, and a lost golden
landscape exchanged for this (then) barren and forbidding
ground. So he gave us the code to enable us to penetrate to
that other "realer" world. Or so I think.

After five more stanzas, a few lines into the sixth and last,
Kaufman ends as follows:

> There's a huge rock lying on my chest And I can't get
> up.

Of course there is the weight of our history, and of her personal choices, but she has got up, over and over, and remains
a grand writer and woman—look up her poem on Lot's wife.

Abba Kovner is worth a book unto himself. He was
one of the leaders of the Vilna ghetto partisans during the
German occupation, and one of the few survivors able to

make a harrowing escape. He still carried all that experience
with him, his face a furrowed map of sadness, despite his
fame and honor as an Israeli poet. At the reception I couldn't
help telling him about an experience I had in Eilat in 1967,
then a frontier town, shortly before the Six-Day War. The
town was a dusty outpost, with a wind-swept, scraggly beach
where Jewish hippies camped out with bottles of Manisch-
ewitz wine, in sight of the Jordan border. And rangy blonde
Israelis came in from King Solomon's Mines not far away
wearing broad brimmed hats, worn khakis, and big pistols
strapped to their hips and thighs. In that milieu, I unexpectedly ran across what looked like a Brooklyn candy store, with
a showcase of knishes out front. When the proprietor, in a
dirty apron and badly in need of a shave, came out, I took
it all in and, quite unbidden, unconsciously, what came out
was Yiddish, which I rarely spoke at that time: *"Vos macht
a Yid du?"* What is a Jew doing in a place like this? *"S'iz a
midbhar!"* I exclaimed. It's a desert! Hearing me telling him
this, Kovner, a devoted Israeli, but not a Sabra, provided the
perfect response, also in Yiddish, speaking for his generation
and their experience: *"Noch vos hut uns getroffen, a Midbhar
passt far Yidn."* After what has happened to us, a desert suits
us Jews. I was and remain humbled and quiet, never doubt-
ing, though often objecting to some official policies, Israel's
right and need to exist.

Joseph Brodsky

Ifirst saw and heard Brodsky for four hours in Peter Viereck's living room when he had just arrived at Mount Holyoke College from Russia. He talked almost continually, with an occasional sardonic grin or tightening of his lips, about the story of his life in the Soviet Union. He grew up in Leningrad (now St. Petersburg again), where his trials for the crimes of being a poet and unemployed were held, and where he was sentenced to years in the gulag cutting down and chopping up frozen trees. These labors were the source of his recurrent heart problems. My first impression during and after that evening was of his inner strength, and of an incandescent idealism, strange and ennobling, so foreign to us living in the privileged West.

I was there with my wife, Anne Halley; Bill McFeeley—an eminent professor of history at Mount Holyoke at the time—and his wife Mary; Peter and his wife. McFeeley and I had signed the papers initiated by Viereck to bring Brodsky out of the Soviet Union and into a visiting Five College teaching position. None of us was then an administrator, high or low, but with sublime chutzpah and Viereck's push and status, the ploy worked and here, indeed, was thin, intense Joseph Brodsky holding forth on his first day in South Hadley! When McFeeley and I occasionally meet these days we agree that those hours were the most moving evening in our academic lives.

That idealism as he spoke of his persecution, the stupid interrogations in Leningrad, the betrayal of other Soviet era writers including some "stars"—the hardships of prison camp, reminded me of accounts I'd read about the "1905-ers." Those were participants in the unsuccessful, but wholly idealistic, failed first Russian revolution. They, too, had withstood extraordinary hardships, but even in defeat most never lost faith in the cause of human liberation. I think Brodsky's sustaining faith was in literature, especially the heroes and martyrs, the real poets of Russia, Anna Akmatova, Osip Mandelstam and his wife Nadezhda, author of the unbearable account of his imprisonment and death, *Hope Against Hope*, and scores of others killed or silenced by Stalin and his apparatchiks. He scorned Yevtushenko as too favored by the regime, despite his brave poem "Babi Yar," that memorialized the thousands of Jews murdered there by the Germans, when it was not fashionable in Communist countries to acknowledge Jews as the primary targets of Nazi barbarity. Yet Yevtushenko somehow survived official censure and was even allowed to go on reading tours to Europe and the U.S. In fact, we saw and heard him read to a full great hall in Tuebingen, Germany in 1963. A celebrity, but no great hero to Brodsky.

Brodsky's career in our country took some surprising turns itself on his way to the Nobel Prize. Shortly after our memorable evening he was supporting Richard Nixon and the continuation of the Vietnam War, stunning his early friends and champions. Many of us did not understand the strength of the anti-Communism of those who had escaped it. Then, too, we heard about his inciting a brawl in a Detroit bar with racist comments. Hearsay, so I make no comment, but he had some turbulent adjustments to make, finally landing on his feet as an admired teacher. He made his students memorize poems, as he had memorized Auden, Donne and many others. He became a prized figure on the New York literary scene, filling out physically, becoming robustly handsome, having fabled romances.

His appearance to the contrary, his health had been broken by those hard years, and he had early heart problems. At a party at Mount Holyoke I reproached him gently for his continued heavy smoking (non-filtered Camels, no less, when he couldn't get Gauloise) and drinking. He waved me off, pooh-poohing it in a very dismissive, fatalistic Russian way. *Nitchie voh.* In the end, he died of that heart disease, too soon, too soon.

As a coda to this story, around the year 2000–2001, my last full year as editor of *MR*, I had to make the round of the colleges supporting us to make sure our subventions would continue, and maybe add a buck or two. With Dan Czitrom, professor of history at Mount Holyoke, as my cicerone, I went to the office of the Provost, Don Shea, to make my pitch. The Provost was a very genial and intelligent man, a fine mathematician and humanist. We got on well, the beneficence for *MR* quickly assured. Then I pointed out that there didn't seem to be any visible sign of Brodsky's important sojourn at the college. Why, for example, no picture of him in that office? The superb photographer from Hampshire College,

Jerome Liebling, had done a wonderful portrait of Brodsky as the cover of an *MR* issue in which an appreciation of Brodsky as teacher had appeared. Why didn't the college purchase a large print from Jerry? After all, how many Nobel Prize winners could they boast of? The long and the short of it is that for a meager six hundred dollars the picture now graces their Library, Mount Holyoke College owning a valuable twofer, two artists honored, the poet and the photographer.

Maishe Mirsky

That's Mark Mirsky. Recently he decided that was what he wanted to be called—his right, and considering the path of his career, probably inevitable. Harvard, the son of Wilfred Mirsky, also Harvard, one of the earliest Jewish representatives (from Dorchester, Mattapan, and Roxbury, the old Boston's Jewish East Side) to the General Court of Massachusetts. Wilfred Mirsky spent his career in that tribal enclave of Irish pols (and a few token Italians, see *The Last Hurrah*, where they would give them "another statue to Columbus"), and summered in Hull, with those pols and retired judges (also pols). Using this leverage, he did push through the first big building program for the University of Massachusetts when he was the first Jew in the legislature to chair its committee on education. Mark inherited that house in Hull, where Anne and I spent some lovely hours, including one memorable Passover seder. It was done in a grand and traditional manner and, because it included his sister and long-standing family conflicts, "a Passover meal with all the fixations" (to quote Diana Trilling about her family seders). I never did go diving in the Bay with Mark/Maishe, though I envied him his daring—he also drove a motorcycle for years, once at least all over Europe, where he visited us in Freiburg and gave Anne a thrill riding up and down the hills of the Schwarzwald. There, too, I was chicken. In short, I grew to

love and admire Mark, from the time we met at the founding
of CCLM, more than any writer I have known.

The "path" of his career should have been predictable.
Early on his was a different voice among Jewish American
writers. Even in the earliest of his seven or eight novels and
story collections the familiar immigrant stories are imbued and
estranged with deep knowledge of the conventional as well as
the arcane aspects of the Jewish tradition. His bent for the
surreal and mystical has often been noted, but it is not an
affectation, as it so often seems to be with other contemporary
writers who suddenly see the potential for what they hope will
be originality in all that. In *Blue Hill Avenue* (1972) the autho-
rial voice asserts that "A mystical doctrine says God exists only
by recognition of the scholars." Mirsky is a scholar as well as a
fiction writer, and he has created God throughout his career,
even when he writes about teaching, lust, and sexual longing.

He devoted years to the study of Kabbalah for hours
every morning before going off to teach at City College.
MR published one of his fine stories about Kabbalah in
the Connecticut Valley, later part of a novel, *The Red Adam*
(1990), that I mention because, aside from its subject matter, it was the first (and maybe the only?) time we printed
a Hebrew letter in the text. Odd, because Leonard Baskin,
who set the tone of *MR's* art and design for years, was a
great lover of the Hebrew alphabet, which appears in many
of his works. Mark's work only got richer and deeper with
the years, and in many forms. He edited a massive history
of Pinsk, his family's home-place in Russia, lengthy and
original studies of Shakespeare and Dante, and much else.

He was a great public reader, having hoped to be an actor in his Harvard years. He dazzled me and an audience at an annual Jewish Studies meeting in Boston when we spoke together about Jewish American literature, and he gave a brilliant twenty minute talk, impromptu because the organizers had changed his subject without informing us prior to our appearance there.

A serious man, as writer, father, teacher, editor of *Fiction*, but a helluva lot of fun, with many writer friends, here and in Europe. It was always worth climbing the long flights to his basic Bowery loft apartment which he and his artist wife Inger (a Norwegian convert to Judaism, and beautiful) continued to live in for years, saving money for the *yeshiva*— and later Williams College and Harvard—education of their gifted son and daughter. One always met interesting people there, with good food, wine, talk throughout an evening. I learned more about Massachusetts and New York politics from Mark than from any other source, and I have been politically active since I was twelve.

All of this praise and appreciation is really prelude to my dissatisfaction with City College's and CUNY's failure to appreciate Mark/Maishe sufficiently. Besides editing *Fiction* from its inception, in the early years with his friend and colleague Donald Barthelme, who did appreciate Mark, and publishing massively, he taught his ass off to generations of students. For several years he directed both the Writing Program and Judaic Studies Program, from the open admission seventies, when he said to me he was "the highest paid junior high school teacher in New York," to the more stimulating later years when he brought, along with dedicated teaching, good writing from talented multi-racial and multi-ethnic students. So what's the beef? A couple of years ago Mark came up for consideration for one of the City University Distinguished Professorships, and I was asked to write a recommendation. I had done one such previously for Morris Dickstein, who got the prized title, and richly deserved it. I wrote an even stronger recommendation for Mark, perhaps too over the top, who was denied it. Shame, City. Maishe Mirsky is a jewel in your crown.

Paolo Milano

That was a name to reckon with, when I first heard it uttered by the *jeunes filles* flitting through the French and Italian hall at Brooklyn College. He was a Jewish Italian exile from Mussolini, publishing in *Partisan Review* and reputedly a devastating ladies' man. He taught at Queens College and occasionally gave a lecture at Brooklyn where the girls, who had given up their neighborhood Jewishness for Proust (well, they kept that version of Jewishness but didn't call attention to it, and accepted Milano's), swooned. Or so I was told, mostly by Mary Doyle Curran, a colleague of his at Queens a little while later. I know Mary thought he was wonderful; anything else at this point is just conjecture.

On my first trip to Italy in 1963, I looked up a colleague in Rome, Joe LoPreato, an anthropologist spending a year there while writing a book on the Calabrian peasantry. He drove me around the town in a Fiat 600, spitting out the shells of fava beans, showing me the landmarks. It was great. We stopped at a famous literary cafe on the Piazza del Popolo where he pointed out the beautiful women and whatever celebrity was present (was one Alberto Moravia?). Suddenly he said, "There goes Paolo Milano!" Where, where? All I saw was his back, ducking quickly around a corner. In pursuit? I was not actually to see him until about fifteen years later.

My wife and I had decided that Rome just had too much

to take in at any one visit, so we tried to see only one Rome at a time: classical Rome; churches and paintings of the counter-Reformation; Hawthorne and James's Rome; Fascist and modern Rome. One year in the late seventies we "did" feminist and Jewish Rome. The entry to the feminist side was literary. Because she herself was a writer and poetry editor of *MR*, women poets and writers were glad to befriend Anne and invited her one night to one of their meetings. One of the women we had met earlier was a Sicilian poet, named something like Femina, with wild, wonderful Circe-like red hair. Those were the days. I drove Anne to the address, parking in a nearby alley for an hour while she met the writers en masse. I sat in the car, closely watched by two police parked right behind me the whole time. I wondered why, then realized: it was still the era of La Lotta Continua, the Red Brigades in Germany, and all that. I sweated it out, Anne returned, and we left without incident. Jewish Rome was more interesting, to me, poignant but less frightening. Sig. Milano was part of that.

At Mark Mirsky's apartment in New York I had met Elena Mortara, a teacher of Jewish American literature at the University of Rome, who was a visiting lecturer for a semester in one of the city colleges. If the name resonates, it is because she is from the Mortara family, one of whose children was kidnapped in the mid-nineteenth century as a young boy by the Catholic Church and raised as a Catholic. The case is still a source of pain and anger in the Italian Jewish community. Her husband was a leader of the Roman Jewish community when we visited there. Elena showed us around including the lovely, classical synagogue, on whose front a tablet recounting the crimes of the Nazis against the Italian Jews is fixed, impossible not to elicit tears (*"Crime horribile"* as Malamud puts it in "The Last Mohican," his best story, set in Rome). I asked if she knew Paolo Milano, who had retired to Rome, and indeed she did. Would she phone him and ask if he would receive us? Yes, and thus it was set up.

We took a streetcar to get to the apartment building, a nice middle-class structure on a busy street. Up the elevator and admitted to the apartment by Milano's man, a gentle six-footer. We took in the elegant two-story apartment before Milano entered from a side room, on the arm of his man. He was surprisingly short, thin and very frail, but with a large, most beautiful head and face. He said he had been ill for a while, and was therefore wearing, as he had for several days, only a bathrobe (quite a nice one), a scarf and slippers. He invited us to sit, asking his valet to bring us a drink—a thimbleful of some liqueur—and dismissed the servant. His first question was what was happening in the literary world of America, which we batted around as well as we could. Mostly we listened to him in fascination. He still reviewed French and Italian books, in his mid-eighties, for the weekly *L'Espresso*, Italy's leading literary journal, but said he always spent two hours a day reading just for pleasure, not on assignment. His wife had left for the US two years previously, so he did not go out much. He was utterly charming as he sat there with his beautiful head, speaking easily and melodiously, and I thought if this fellow were ten years younger I would really worry about his seducing Anne. She agreed when we discussed it later.

Finally, he said, "Now I want to show you my shame," and rose to go open the door to what he said was his bedroom. I wondered, migod, is this going to be a "Rose for Emily" situation, with something bizarre and/or truly shameful in there? What there was were two twin beds. One bed, he said, was where he slept; on the other were piles and piles of books in three languages. "These," he said, "are the books I haven't read."

Edward Dahlberg

Dahlberg has been called a sport of American literature, as indeed he was. He has also been called the Job of that literature, and in his late works, a great stylist (by Allen Tate). He went from an early thirties naturalistic style, politically left, though not dogmatically or egregiously so, but writing in a slangy vernacular about Bottom Dogs, and earning the praise of even D.H. Lawrence. Then on to a wildly baroque, some would say ornate and affected high style, full of classical and Biblical allusions, pre-Columbian esoterica, raunchy aphorisms and tales (in books called *The Sorrows of Priapus*, *The Carnal Myth*, *The Flea of Sodom*) reminiscent of a tradition from the classics through the Renaissance, and who knows what else, but highly original. A sport. You either fell under his spell and loved the wild ride of his prose, or you shunned or ignored it.

I first learned of Dahlberg when I returned East to teach at an open admissions part of Boston University in 1956. It was a terrible place, basically a cash-cow junior college for the university, in which we slaveys taught fifteen hours, lectured often to 125 students at a clip, in classes from which they tended to drop like flies. The faculty, however, was full of interesting souls, dedicated and very good teachers for the most part. One of them a few years before I got there had been, defying belief, Edward Dahlberg. One present colleague had been an acolyte, and from him I heard my first Dahlbergism: "Naturalism is matter in motion loathing itself."

From then on, I paid attention whenever his name came up. As it did in a little magazine, short lived, but wonderful, called *First Person*, edited out of Rockport, Massachusetts by M. D. Elevitch, who had been a classmate at Minnesota and was a founding spirit of the Association of Little Magazines of America. Also a literary sport, author of two strange but interesting novels, he published some of Dahlberg's autobiographical *Because I Was Flesh*.

When I became editor of *The Massachusetts Review*, Dahlberg was definitely on my radar, and we published him several times. The first piece, in 1962, was also autobiographical, about the life he lived as the bastard son of his lady barber mother Lizzie and his painful sense of fatherlessness. That piece ends with, for me, a heartbreakingly beautiful tribute to his mother after her death (which also ends *Because I Was Flesh*): "When the image of her comes up on a sudden just as my bad demons do and I see again her dyed henna hair, the eyes dwarfed by the electric lights in the Star Lady Barbershop, and the dear, broken wing of her mouth, and when I regard her wild tatters, I know that not even Solomon in his lilied raiment was so glorious as my mother in her rags." Inspired by a passage in Hamlet, pointed out to me by my colleague David Clark, in which that errant son refuses to say good night to Claudius, presumptive father, because, since in marriage mother and father are one, he will simply only have to say, logic-chopping like a good student from Wittenberg, good night to his mother alone, "And so my mother," he says, and that was the title I gave the piece.

It came back to haunt me. In an essay I later wrote about Dahlberg's early and late work, I said something like Dahlberg's search for America was tied in with his relationship to his mother and their Midwestern hegira, an Oedipal drive of sorts. Well, Dahlberg invited me to come see him when I was in New York on some occasion, so on a mild autumn night I took a cab from my midtown hotel up to his apartment, I think in the west 80s off Central Park. He and his lovely blonde English wife greeted me at the door very warmly, smiling broadly. Edward and I went immediately into his study—piled high with books, but in a kind of graduate school set of, for the most part, orange crates. He never did get rich, was really one of those who lived for his writing. He was in a stylishly heavy brocaded bathrobe, however, with a white foulard around his neck, and as we settled down, his wife brought us tea and discreetly left. At which point, Dahlberg stared at me with his one good eye (the other was glass) and said, "An Oedipal impulse? Sleep with my mother? The thought never entered my mind!" Taken aback, I sat there dumbfounded, listening for the next hour and a half to an incredible monologue about his life, his work, his grievances with other writers who tended to make all kinds of ignorant mistakes, and betrayals, the difficulties of his writing meaningfully ("I have to read entire books at times"—he was then into pre-Columbian civilizations and myths—"to get one good sentence written").

I stumbled out of the apartment, walking the forty or

fifty blocks back to my hotel, to clear my head. From then on, whenever I wrote a recommendation for Dahlberg, at his request, for a Guggenheim or an NEA grant, I always sent him a copy, not wanting him ever to accuse me of stabbing him in the back. I continued to read and admire him, but we never met or even corresponded again, though *MR* did publish more of his work.

Paul Goodman

Peter Rose, a long-time professor of sociology at Smith College, and I spent a good hour walking the streets of Northampton on a bitter cold winter evening in the late sixties with Paul Goodman, who had spoken earlier at the college. A slight figure, he was wearing what we used to call a "pupke" hat—woolen, with a small ball of wool on top—pulled over his ears, hunched over against the cold, his nose running a little, until we ended up at a scruffy old-time diner, talking for hours.

What I remember most is his comparing New York Puerto Ricans with the city's urban blacks. A frequent player of playground handball, that grand city game, he noted that when a ball went astray the Puerto Rican kids would stop it and return it to the players; the black kids simply let it go by them. As an occasional volunteer worker in the city hospitals, he also observed that black patients were often alone, occasionally visited by one family member. The Puerto Ricans were usually surrounded by family, bearing food, drinks, flowers; if one of them opened a bodega or other small business, in the city or in its suburbs, family and friends rallied around, at least for a while, as customers or supporters.

He worried about what he perceived as a breakdown in the African American family and in community coherence and pride—a kind of social pathology made famous or infamous by Moynihan and Glazer. One can challenge these generalizations, and the reliability of such a small and idiosyncratic sampling. Forty years on, one cannot totally romanticize Puerto Rican solidarity and community values, parts of it in disarray in the communities of Holyoke, Springfield, some of New York, where their socio-economic condition remains low, for the most part, though the brilliant career and rise of Judge Sotomayor may be a harbinger and sign of better conditions. Black life has certainly picked up on many fronts—the election and presidency of Barack Obama is a major cause for hope—but the inner cities are still what they are, if not worse than forty years ago, as *The Wire*, that fine television series on HBO, and much other testimony would have us believe.

Goodman had a sharp eye about so much of American reality.

No one can deny his prescience about the failures in American education, chronicled by him in *Growing Up Absurd* (1960) and *Compulsory Mis-education* (1964). He anticipated and spoke for the sixties youth critique and rebellion. He has sometimes been called "the philosopher of the New Left," especially after the paperback version of his *Making Do* (1963) was so widely read and influential. Prior to these significant books, in a story called "A Memorial Synagogue," (begun in 1935, completed in 1947) reprinted in *Jewish American Literature: a Norton Anthology* (2001), he memorialized in original and arresting fashion the disasters of the Jewish people—and all other peoples—years before the full dimension of the Shoah became known. His extraordinary trilogy, *The Empire City* (1942, 1946, 1950), with its hero named Horatio Alger negotiating New York City through the forties, remains a great read. Funny and/or shocking to some, wise to others, he shows how Horatio learns math, geography, history in the subway system; how anarchist communes fail because they don't solve the problem of who takes out the garbage. Horatio participates in progressive, Dewey/Reichian-inspired pre-schools, in which stark-naked children paddle across the floor and each other. And more.

Dead in 1972 at 60, his health perhaps affected terribly by the death, shortly before, of a beloved son in a mountain climbing accident, his productivity in a variety of fields and forms was enormous. Philosophical anarchist, free spirit, bisexual (which got him canned from several colleges before mores changed and became more forgiving), he published some forty books of verse, drama, stories, essays on architecture—*Communitas* with his brother Percival Goodman—and a pioneering work on Gestalt psychology with Fritz Perls. He even earned a doctorate at the University of Chicago with an Aristotelian dissertation on form in literature (which I have read and was impressed by). His books are still available through alternative presses, but he is too little known and honored these days, though assuredly he should be.

Norman Podhoretz brags about his liberal bona fides, as prelude to his seeing the light and turning away from those misguided ideas of his youth, towards neo-con-dom, when in his first days as editor of *Commentary* in the early sixties, he published the seemingly outrageous and radical work of Paul Goodman and Norman Mailer. And see where he and his journal ended up when they stopped all that.

Ruth Whitman—
Translations &
Transformations

In 1957, living in Cambridge, Massachusetts while work-ing at Boston University, I took a summer course in Greek at Harvard, so that I could use the Widener Library the rest of the year and finish my dissertation. Next door to my class an eminent Classics professor named Cedric Whitman was teaching. That induced me to attend a poetry reading by Ruth Whitman, who had been married to him and bore his name, but, as it turned out when we met and talked, she was now married to Firman Houghton (of the Houghton-Mifflin connection), with whom she was running a small literary mag-azine. I only learned she was Jewish when in 1966 I reviewed a volume of her translations of Yiddish poetry—which in my view she did very well—in *The Nation*. She was by then no longer with Houghton. She was beautiful, ardent, and a fine poet. She did many more translations from the Yiddish besides publishing her own verse in English. I corresponded and caught glimpses of her occasionally while I was at *MR*, but she has passed away, in 1999 at the age of 77. Her coming from such mainstream marriages and other similar connec-tions to Yiddish poetry makes me wonder about so many transformations, and Jewish self-discovery, as it were, among well-known and honored men and women poets (John Hollander and Adrienne Rich come to mind), critics like Irving Howe, who co-edited with Eliezer Greenberg two significant volumes of Yiddish poets and fiction writers that remain the best in the field—especially Howe's long introductions, which are must reading. Howe had made a name early in his career with volumes on Faulkner and Thomas Hardy, mainline decidedly non-Jewish writers. Of course, there is Saul Bellow's transformative translation—for him, Singer, and American letters—of Isaac Bashevis Singer's "Gimpel the Fool."

There are scores of lesser-known writers who have trod this path and who are more than just interesting footnotes to a trend. There is a serious social implication to all of these translators from one world to another and their intellectual and creative transformations. I think of former students and/or colleagues of mine: Marcia Falk, who did a splendid translation in book form of The Song of Songs, and now teaches mostly Jewish subjects; Jyl Felman, a fine gay Jewish poet and prose writer—her memoir *Cravings* is a delight, about growing up Jewish in echt straight and middle-America Dayton, Ohio; Lev Raphael, another gay poet and story writer, author of *Dancing on Tisha B'Ov* (a collection of stories about gay life, Jewish and otherwise, that can still shock and inform me). Former colleagues John Clayton, who began writing about the New Left, and Jay Neugeboren, who began as a wonderful writer about sports, are now both prize-winners for their stories about Jewish American life.

There is also the amazing case of Aaron Lansky, a young graduate of the Yiddish program under Ruth Wisse in

Montreal, whom I didn't know when he appeared in my office a couple of decades ago. He came to ask me to sign a letter requesting money from a Jewish foundation. For what? To collect Yiddish language books that might be headed for oblivion and house them in Amherst. A Yiddish book collection? In Amherst of all places? Why? Well, he explained, because he liked the town, having graduated from Hampshire College a few years earlier. Okay, that was an honest response. I glanced at the letter, which already had Irving Howe and Saul Bellow as signatories. In that case, why not—I added my name, never expecting to see Lansky again. Boy, was I wrong! From the humblest of beginnings, he was instrumental in creating a magnificent institution, the National Yiddish Book Center, getting land from Hampshire College, thousands of contributors, and a wonderful building, one of the most beautiful in town. It attracts tens of thousands of visitors a year, and oh yes, it has millions of books in its possession—saved from that threatening oblivion. Lansky richly deserved his MacArthur Fellowship, granted a few years ago. The Institute also helps train and inspire whole new generations of young American Jews eager to connect with this part of their Jewish past. Lansky's book, *Outwitting History*, about his *zamling* (collecting) is full of wonderful stories, too, and well worth reading. I am proud to have served twice on the Institute's Board of Directors.

There is, however, one of the earliest and best translators of Yiddish poetry who is closest to my heart: Sarah Zweig Betsky, whose book *Onions and Cucumbers and Plums: 46 Yiddish Poems in English* (the title comes from a refrain in a poem by M. L. Halpern) she edited and translated during the Second World War as a master's thesis. It was published by Wayne State University Press in 1958, followed by a new edition in 1980. It is a beautifully designed book, with an impeccable selection of poets and poems, all in the original Hebrew lettering, also transliterated into Roman lettering, and then into English. Betsky's story starts for me when in 1977 I was asked to take over a graduate course at Yale in nineteenth-century American literature and culture for a semester. Its regular professor, R. W. B. Lewis, had just won a National Book Award for his work on Edith Wharton and had taken off for Italy. Who can blame him? After my introductory lecture an attractive young woman student came up to me and said, "You look just like my uncle Sam." That got my attention. She then told me about herself and her family. Her name was Ceil, she had come to graduate school at Yale from the Netherlands, where her mother and father, Sarah and Seymour Betsky, were professors at different Dutch universities. I remembered Leslie Fiedler telling me he couldn't offer me a job in the English department at the University of Montana, where he was then chairman, because there were already too many Jews in the department, including Seymour Betsky. I refrained from telling Ceil that Fiedler story. She said that her mother was coming to visit her in a couple of weeks, and would I like to meet her? Absolutely—so there I was in a Yale dining hall, waiting for them to appear at the appointed day and hour. As they approached, I exclaimed to the mother, "You look just like my Aunt Sarah!" When it turned out her maiden name was Zweig, the deal was closed.

It was also my mother's (and her sister Sarah's) maiden name. So, though her family came form Lvov *gebernye* (district) and my mother's from the Lubline *gebernye*, which are actually not that far apart in southern Poland, we decided we must be cousins, however distant or close. We haven't had our DNAs checked, but I still consider us family.

At least twice we met in Europe, once early in 1978 in Germany, in our temporary house in Freiburg, where they arrived in a terrible storm and had a terrible marital quarrel; once in their home in the Netherlands, where they had a superb collection of Dutch genre paintings. I was there because in 1980 I was a finalist for the Chair in Amsterdam University, no doubt due to Sarah (who was not, however, a professor at Amsterdam). In the Betskys's home town in Holland we even ate at a restaurant where the Crown Prince was wont to eat. In Freiburg I had told them about my first interview for a job with Fiedler. "Oh!" she exploded, "He's such a *ligner!*" What? What exactly do you mean? Such a liar! You mean they weren't picketed by the American Legion?, or that there weren't too many Jews in their department? She didn't answer. Her bitter tone implied that there was more to it than that. I never fathomed the reasons, but suspect they felt the Betskys might have done better to stay in the States—although they had excellent positions and a good life, it seemed to me—if Leslie had been of more help to them. Or it may be due to her disapproval of the way the Fiedlers raised their many kids—the apparent chaos, the later pot-smoking scandal Leslie got into and out of in Buffalo. Just conjectures, from a distance, when it no longer matters.

Seymour has since died. Sarah tried after that, unsuccessfully, to get a job and return to the United States. The last time I saw her, at an National Book Awards ceremony, Ceil worked in publishing in New York. Sarah and her excellent book and her work lives. And I love you, my cousin. All my cousins.

Harvey Swados

I got a phone call one day in the late sixties from Ben Seligman, the first director of the recently established Labor Relations and Research Center at the University of Massachusetts. We knew and were friendly with each other because of one of those small-world, certainly in academia, situations. Not always an academic, Ben had come to us from Washington, where he had been a New Dealer and important in the world of labor legislation. His wife Libby had been executive secretary of a Jewish NGO in D.C.—where her secretary had been Beatie Raskin, a beloved cousin of mine. So they had called when they came to Amherst, and in time, their two children became enmeshed in our lives to some degree. Their daughter worked for us at *The Massachusetts Review* while she was a student, before going on to an academic career in North Carolina; and their son, Rafael Mevorach (he had changed his name when he was a kibbutznik in Israel, after attending Hampshire College) earned a doctorate in Music Composition at the University of Nebraska. Last year Rafael appeared at my door unexpectedly, as was his wont, to ask if it was all right to use a poem of Anne's in a cantata he was working on. Did he need to ask? Ben and Libby have long since passed on, and I think Rafael and I both value this connection with each other's past.

So Ben called me, that 1960s day, to say that his friend (from earlier Shachtmanite days, I believe), Harvey Swados, was tired of teaching at Sarah Lawrence—for one thing, they didn't pay much and he had a family to support. Could I see if we could bring him to the university's English Department? I leaped at the idea, having known and cherished Swados's work for years. Many of his books are still on my shelves. I gave some of them recently to Robert Niemi, a former graduate student now professor at St. Michael's College in Vermont, who was producing a Swados monograph for the American Writers Series.

I was and am especially grateful for *On the Line*, fourteen stories about assembly line factory workers based on Harvey's own years of work at various times in factories at skilled and unskilled labor. Published in 1957, the year before I came to UMass, it was about real working class jobs in our country at mid-century, and the emotional and physical price they exacted: unsentimentalized, honest, and at bottom sympathetic to a world scarcely recognized or written about in the mainstream literature of the period. Harvey was extraordinarily productive in the years before that call from Seligman. The works I treasured were *Nights in the Gardens of Brooklyn* (given its title and subject, his New York days) in 1960; *Years of Conscience: The Muckrakers—an Anthology of Reform Journalism* (1961), a collection I used for years in my classes on American life and culture between the Civil War and World War I; and *Standing Fast* (worked on for several years and published in 1970). There were many others stories, memoirs, novels, that had received varying critical and commercial success.

I cite these works and Harvey's productivity—and I could mention as well his recognition in the literary world of the time as one among writers like Bellow and Philip Roth, although not as commercially successful as they—because when I approached the director of our MFA Program about Swados, he had never heard of him. I proceeded to educate him (tactfully), gave him things to read, and in those days before having to be vetted by PC administrative rules, Harvey got the job offer. One of the few times I would justify an Old Boys network! First he was a visiting professor, but in the next year, 1970, he became a tenured professor, teaching fiction writing, and moved his family to the region.

He liked being here and the students loved him: he was a warm and carefully attentive, responsible teacher. And not just to the students: Jay Neugeborn, for one, also in the program, looked upon him as a mentor and model, as well as friend. The MFA director came to be his close friend and greatest admirer.

We had a good relationship that included a memorable dinner party at our house with him, his lovely wife Bette, and another writer, an incredibly successful one, non-academic, with books on language and on North American Indians, who had taken up residence in our town, along with his gracious wife and family there to attend to his every need. His books were well-written, about difficult matter, in an impressively comprehensible way—to me they were like the best term papers one could ever produce, but they made the writer a small fortune. Which he liked to talk about, at length, for example at a New Year's Eve dinner party with Lisa and Leonard

Baskin, one of the most uncomfortable evenings of its kind in my life. At the conclusion of the meal at our house, the other couple left first, and Harvey then said to us: "This is the second time I have been to dinner with that guy. Don't ever invite me with him again!" And we never did.

There were occasions at which I marveled at his expert knowledge of French wine, enjoying the way he lovingly handled a bottle, uncorked it, and then savored the flavors as he swirled a mouthful. He was indeed a man who loved life. He and his family had spent much time in the south of France, on sabbaticals and years of grant awards, but alas, only a short time teaching in Amherst. Harvey died, suddenly, while painting the bathroom of his house, of an aneurism, in 1972, at the age of 52. The shock of that still reverberates, for his family—of whom I knew best only his son Robin, an actor who had the lead in a university production of *Company*—and those of us who knew or studied with him. At his memorial service at the university, I spoke of what his work had meant for me, a liberation of sorts in that earlier buttoned up period. His was a unique and strong voice: Harvey Swados had always stood fast. He is missed, and needed.

Clara & Richard Winston

Early upon our arrival in Amherst, we were invited for drinks to the home—an Amherst College apartment, really—of Bill and Mary Heath. He was a young assistant professor of English, as I was at the University, who was to remain for years at the College as a beloved teacher. Mel, as Mary was always called, and my wife Anne had been recruited by Leo Marx to be graders for him in American Studies. And so we met and became lifelong friends, Mel ultimately working at every position at *The Massachusetts Review*, including years as senior editor, a job she loved, as she said, and what she had always wanted to do. At that late afternoon hour Ben and Peggy Demott were present, as were Clara Winston and her husband, Richard.

I mention all this because Demott, even then a well-known literary light, announced in his usual assured manner that Anne was the best poet in the Pioneer Valley, and Clara Winston was the best prose writer. Neither Anne nor I knew at the time who Clara was, nor had we read a word she had written. After such high praise, not too long afterwards, we did read her three novels, *The Closest Kin There Is*, *The Hours Together*, and *Painting for the Show*. We had to agree with the high estimate of Clara, certainly about *The Hours Together*, an extraordinary and moving story, too little known these days, about a German Jewish refugee couple in New York, their therapy and their deaths. The feeling, the sharply observed detail, are palpable and brilliant as when the couple visit the Metropolitan Museum and are overcome by a painting of the Crucifixion: "Imagine, real nails, through human flesh."

The first novel was about incest in rural New England, feelingly told and sensitive, too, but not up to *The Hours Together*, and *Painting for the Show* had a rather nasty view of an artist whose abstract expressionism was just an instrument for commercial success; and there is even some unlikely Mafia involvement in the whole sordid thing. That book was published only in England, not finding an American publisher, despite the great talent the writer had displayed in her previous book, which had also received good reviews. A sad commentary on American publishing, even worse now in its all-out commercialism, where many well-published serious writers are finding it difficult to get work accepted.

All of this is important to recount, recover, and celebrate, but what is most interesting to me is, in effect, the interesting "back story" of the lives they led. They had been pacifists, New Yorkers, before America entered World War II, and had decided in 1940 to abandon the city and the dominant politics of their time. They would try to make a go of hardscrabble subsistence farming in Vermont, while also leading a literary life they saw as their real vocation. A familiar dream to many over the years, but they did it, striking out with little money, city folks braving a tough farm life. The farm, right over the border from Massachusetts, was ultimately a lovely place and piece of land, which they named Duino

Farm, honoring the great German poet Rilke, author of *The Duino Elegies*. Richard became a major translator of German literature, occasionally of Thomas Mann, and other lesser or equal eminences, as well as an accomplished historian. He and Clara worked very assiduously at these translations, a hard way to make a living, but essential to supplement the meager farm income. Richard told me he had milked their cow twice daily, and rather missed it when they were able to devote full time to literary pursuits. We had many lovely dinners and occasions there; they were lavishly hospitable.

The reason they had been in Amherst where we met them is that at a certain point, their two daughters needed a better high school than rural Vermont offered, so they moved to our town for the winters (not always a pleasure on the farm in any case). These girls were extraordinary; they would excuse themselves from a dinner to go up and read the Latin and German classics they so enjoyed, and not because they were school assignments. They thought that was the most natural thing in the world, didn't everyone do the same? No. Christina became a Classics professor at Smith, and her older sister a professor of German at Wesleyan. Richard also instructed Anne about her translations: it's okay, he said, to improve the text if it needed it—a literary man, of wide sympathies, not a narrow pedagogue. Clara seemed solemn behind her large strong glasses, with her quietly observing manner, but she had style in her dress, and displayed a wicked wit when it was called for, and of course great intelligence. And they were great cooks.

They both died of cancer, Richard first, Clara a few short

years later. I ran into her at a super market when she had her head in a kerchief, having undergone radiation—brave and resolute to the end, as Stina (Christina) was to inform me. But the horror of their early deaths, so close to each other, may be connected with that cow and the milk Richard so lovingly collected. Who now remembers the Strontium 90 scare of the fifties? That is, when radiation from the nuclear bomb tests in the west floated over parts of the entire country, even, as we now suspect, over the area of Duino Farm. There was concern expressed at the time about its contaminating many things, especially milk, if I remember correctly. Is it too far-fetched to consider these peaceful, principled anti-war, devotedly humanist writers casualties of the nuclear madness?

Melvin Jules Bukiet, etc.

Ido not know Melvin Jules Bukiet very well, though I have met him twice, and we published his story "The Library of Moloch" in the *Norton Anthology*. The tale, practically allegorical, involves a librarian who compulsively tapes and collects oral testimonies by thousands of survivors of the Shoah, in his own selfish search for life's meaning. Bukiet himself is a son of survivors. The library goes up in flames when the collector drowses off and drops an ash from his cigarette on some inflammable stuff. Certainly a cautionary tale, told with great feeling for the survivors' stories, and great wryness about the academic Holocaust industry. But that is ancillary to my bringing him into my story.

The four editors of the *Anthology* agreed that this was a first-rate piece, original, intellectually significant, a good read well done. Another post-Holocaust tale, also by the son of survivors, was up for consideration, too, about a character who becomes catatonic in an elevator, which to him is transformed into one of the cattle-cars used to transport Jews to the death camps. I had met the author at a Jewish literary conference and liked him, and the story (well enough). The others thought it was too mechanical, forced by an idea, arbitrary, etc. And we had already accepted Bukiet's piece. One of my colleagues was on the fence, and

I thought another could be persuaded to come around and accept—after all, two about this horrendous subject would not be too much. But then a funny thing happened on the way to acceptance: a campaign was launched by friends of this author, also an editor of a Jewish publication, writing letters to us about why we should accept his story. That did it—no one wanted that kind of pressure, log-rolling, or whatever, and we all got our dander up, and that was that. Another cautionary tale, if not about a truly important subject.

Bukiet, Mark Mirsky, Charles Bernstein (also in the *Anthology*) and I did a panel of readings together in D.C. at a Jewish Center, flogging the *Anthology*, and I got to hear Bernstein read one of his language poems, where words and their combinations, and how they were read, rather than essential meanings were the chief concern. It was a tour de force, a string of lines from many other writers that was scintillating. I also learned that he was the son of another kind of survivor: his father was the Hollywood and television writer blacklisted in the McCarthy era, whose story became the basis for the role Woody Allen played in *The Front*. One of Allen's few, if any other, overtly political films, and a terrific one.

But Bukiet is in these narratives for one more, to me, interesting experience. He is a friend of two of my favorite young writers, intellectuals, friends. Val Vinokurov appeared at our door in Amherst one day, shortly after he began his freshman year at Amherst College. He looked like a *yeshiva bocher*, jet-black crop of lank hair and long sideburns. He was, indeed, very religious at the time, and had won a prize for a poem about the new Holocaust Memorial statue in Miami Beach—a long, green hand pointing to the sky, with apparently human figures clinging to the fingers, one of the worst Holocaust memorials I have ever seen. But it had been seen in the local newspaper by a poet we knew and had published in *MR* and she had suggested he come to see us. The first time in all my life a kid had actually done that. And so Val became a member of our family.

He had been brought from Moscow as a five-year-old by his mother, leaving the physician father, and brought up in the very Jewish Miami Beach and its school system. Another young person had also been brought to Miami (not the Beach) at a young age, by her Haitian parents after several years of her Protestant minister father's exile in Fontainebleau. She, Rose Réjouis, went to a Miami high school, deep in the Haitian neighborhood. Neither would have met the other in a million years. But a recruiter for Amherst College had the wit to bring these two promising young people to Amherst on a scholarship. Where they met early on, fell in love and married in their senior year. Anne and I were their witnesses at the Justice of the Peace wedding. Both received scholarships to Princeton, Ph.D.s, and teach now, Comparative Literature and French, at Lang College of the New School. They won prizes for their translations of the patois novels of the Martinique writer Patrick Chamoiseau, as well as publishing their own criticism, verse and fiction.

They had a child five years ago, a boy they named Elia, after Val's Russian Jewish grandfather, who lost a lung at the great tank battle of Kursk in World War II and who died in Russia at the age of 55. I was honored to be asked to be the *sandek* for Elia's *bris*. That is the role of the eldest man, usually the *zayde* (grandfather), of the family, who holds the eight-day old child on his lap, to be prayed over and handed to the *mohel* who performs the circumcision. So there I was in a Brooklyn apartment, sitting at the kitchen table with the boy on a cushion on my lap, friends, including Melvin Jules Bukiet, and Rose's parents, looking on.

The rabbi, as I assumed he must be, though that is not always the case—Anne's grandfather in Bremerhaven had been the Cantor, not the Rabbiner, as well as the *mohel* and ritual slaughterer of the Jewish community there—was an elderly man who carefully laid out on a cloth on the table a surprisingly full array of knives, scissors, tweezers and other implements. He then took the cushion and baby, telling me to hold and press back the child's legs, almost as one would a chicken, and began snipping and cutting, bloodily, for what seemed to me an agonizingly long time. Elia screamed, Rose almost fainted, her mother winced, and I looked on, horrified. My three sons had all been circumcised in hospitals by physicians, and I had never before been so close to the operation (well, once before). My first thought was, "What a barbaric custom!"

An article in the *Forward* (June 5, 2009, p.18) under the headline "Reluctant Mitzvah: A Rabbi Struggles With Her Son's Circumcision," more or less reports the same initial response by a woman rabbi, and other women (one of whom said "No one tells you how terrible it is"). The Rabbi had "wept her way through the service and circumcision," although she comes to see it as a great blessing, "with his *bris* a distant memory for us both," to bring her son "into the covenant of Abraham."

We all got over it, in our own ways. Half ironically, I said to Bukiet, "If I knew this was how it was done to me, I never would have let them do it!" He merely smiled, apparently thinking nothing was amiss. He then told me about the Rabbi who had circumcised one of his sons at the Bukiet home. After the operation, the Rabbi carefully put the snippet of foreskin into a napkin and put it in his bag. When Melvin asked him what he was doing that for, the Rabbi said he always did it, especially on that street, a fashionable tree-lined one on the upper West Side of Manhattan. He had performed many *brises* there, and always planted the foreskins he saved at the base of different trees. I suppose he was trying ultimately to sanctify them all. Do the other residents know they are surrounded by these signs of the Covenant, Chosen, even if not Jewish, through the pain and blood of the Child?

Julius Lester

Speaking of circumcision... Julius Lester worked with me for two years, 1981–83, as Associate Director of the Institute for Advanced Study in the Humanities at the University of Massachusetts Amherst, of which I was the director. When Julius won an award as the best teacher in the Commonwealth a few years later, he said at a public celebration of the honor, that those two years were the best years he had while at the University. I was gratified by that, but a little surprised. Julius was an excellent partner in the enterprise, but he was also a very private person, who never accepted, until years later, any invitation to my house, nor did he ever invite me to cross his threshold. The news he surprised me with towards the end of his stint at the Institute will illustrate what I mean.

On that occasion, he told me in a private tête-à-tête that he had been taking instruction in Hebrew and Judaism for two years with Rabbi Yechiel Lander, Jewish Chaplain at Smith and Amherst. And that he was becoming a Jew. Wow! And never a hint for two years! Lester was the son of a black Protestant minister in the south, a graduate of Fisk himself, and stung in the late 1960s, during the Ocean Hill-Brownsville fracas, with an accusation of anti-Semitism because on his popular NYC radio talk program he had remained silent while a young black student had read a blatantly anti-Jewish poem. This was, therefore, surprising news indeed. I must add that I never thought he was anti-Semitic, not for a moment, ever, and that he had probably been shocked by that recitation, but was abiding by his policy of hands-off, free speech for everyone, not appreciating the volatile quality of the issue. As he was a deeply sensitive and spiritual person, I expect the reaction to that incident began his long path to conversion. Continuing the conversation about his becoming a Jew, he said, "I'm not coming into work tomorrow—I'm going to be circumcised." Staring wide-eyed at the 40-year-old man, about to be "cut" as Jews used to say about the *bris*, all I could say was, "Take the week off." Which he did.

How and when did I get to know Julius Lester? It began with his terrific, immensely favorable, two-page review in *The New York Times Book Review* of *Black and White in American Culture: Ten Years of The Massachusetts Review*, that I and Sidney Kaplan had edited in 1969. How could I not love the guy! I inquired about him from Mike Thelwell, my dear friend and chairman of the African-American Studies Department, recently created, largely through the efforts of Thelwell and Kaplan. Actually, the name of the department was the W. E. B. DuBois Department of African American Studies. It took courage and political wisdom to invoke Dubois's name at that time, unlike Gates's and Harvard's using the name some safe years later. But that's another story. Mike filled me in on Julius, with whom he had worked in SNCC in 1964, assuring me he was an all right guy (I will not use the Mafia term, "a stand-up guy," but it amounts to the same thing).

About a year later, Julius submitted a story to *MR*—

about a black student at a college like Fisk who had to decide between an academic life and activism in the Movement. It ends in standard thirties-type fashion with the student walking up a flight of stairs, not down, and so we know, as certain as day follows night, that he has chosen activism. Not the greatest story, but decent and useful. I was bothered by the language he put into the mouth of a white professor and adviser of his, which seemed stilted and artificial, not apparently the purpose of the writer. So I called Julius and made a date to see him at the Chelsea, where he lived at the time, to discuss the story.

Sitting in the lobby of the Chelsea I presented my concern about that language. Lester said, but that's the way he talked. I asked who he was, and was told it was Professor Bernard Spivack, an eminent Shakespeare scholar, and a cherished mentor to Julius. I said, "Oh my god! Bernard has been a colleague of mine in our English Department for several years—and though I respect, like and admire him, that is the way he talks!" I did add, it's not enough, or esthetically sound, however, to be so totally faithful that it sounds fake! The difficult trick is to show it is stilted but not be stilted. Anyway, he made a little change here and there and we did publish the story, his first, I believe, in a national journal. Since then he has published numerous books: novels, memoirs, children's books of distinction. To Bernard, who died a few years ago, my apologies, and *alav ha-shalom*.

A couple of years later Mike recruited Julius to his department, and there the plot thickens. He worked for years there, teaching about the Civil Rights Movement and other important subjects. About the time he converted to Judaism, James Baldwin appeared to teach for three years, at the initiative primarily of the University, in the Five College Consortium, which included a year of teaching at UMass, and living in Amherst. He then gave a large lecture course in the Civil Rights Movement and was otherwise active on our campus, talking once to two thousand students at our Student Union with Leonard Baskin on "Art and Society." Students, mostly black, lined up during the question period all the way down the hall, and nodded at all his responses (which frankly I did not always grasp, though the empathy in the voice and body language were quite evident to the questioners). When I drove John Wideman to our campus for his job interview with the English Department, I pointed to the building in which Baldwin was at that very moment giving a lecture. Wideman, of course, wanted to stop and go to hear him, which we did. John said afterward that was one good reason for his accepting our offer—"When a man stands up there and says, 'Then I said to Martin,' or 'That's what Malcolm said to me,' I pay attention!" But Julius was critical of Baldwin, mostly for his late nights and what seemed like his not working steadily at his writing.

Baldwin did drink a lot of Scotch (Johnny Walker Black) at some of those evenings downtown and in friends' houses—mostly with good talk all around with his companions—but so did almost every major American writer over many previous decades (think Faulkner, Hemingway, Fitzgerald, Anderson, Dreiser, et al., who did not only drink but were certified alcoholics). And Baldwin did produce works almost to the very end that are the most consequential of his generation. Even if Julius might have been right, which is not a sure thing, it was not a position to endear him to his colleagues. The situation became critical when in one of Baldwin's lectures, some Jewish students in the class thought he had made some anti-Jewish remarks and were deeply disturbed by it. Julius agreed with them and the campus was roiled for weeks, making the local and state newspapers. Fortunately there was a recording and a transcript of the event, which I read, and didn't think his remarks were anti-Semitic—just allusions to the familiar, and historically accurate, animus blacks in Harlem felt at the almost entirely white, including Jewish, ownership of the local shops and stores. That same resentment was felt and acted upon later towards Asian shopkeepers in Los Angeles and elsewhere. But the issue brought to a head Lester's increasing alienation from his department, members of which did in fact think his conversion was odd. Julius complained that he was being made fun of and ultimately "shunned" by his colleagues. And so, finally, a transfer was arranged, satisfactory to all parties, to the Judaic Studies Department, where Julius taught large classes with enormous success and appreciation, for decades, until his retirement.

That's a long accounting, which may have omitted or treated reductively relevant facts, but it is how I saw it then and see it now. It is not the final word on Julius (and me). My wife died after a short illness in the summer of 2004, and was buried in Wildwood Cemetery in Amherst—the most beautiful in the area. On short notice, mostly by word of mouth, about 150 people showed up, men and women, of many ages and many races and backgrounds, including Julius Lester. Hillel Rabbi Saul Perlmutter, who was going to do the graveside service, saw him on the sidelines and asked me if we should ask Julius to do the *El Moleh Rachamim*, the great funeral prayer for God's mercy. I said absolutely. Besides being a wonderful folk singer in his youth, for most years since his conversion he had been a cantor at several synagogues in the area and in New Hampshire. Julius asked for five minutes to look over the Hebrew text, which Saul gave to him. To make an already long story short, he sang it in his beautiful, full, deep voice more movingly than all those present familiar with the *Rachamim* had ever heard it sung before. Yes, there were tears. I thought he was great, and I was immensely grateful.

And finally, Julius came to my house, for the *shiva*, where we talked for an hour. He came again for another hour after that was all over. And since then we have met for lunch often. I still haven't been to his house, but that's all right.

Nat Hentoff
& Others

Nat Hentoff, Harvey Swados, Kenneth Rexroth, and I were the white guys, as I remember it, at a very interesting conference on black writers, early on, in 1963, sponsored by the University of California/Berkeley at Asilomar in California. Upon assuming editorship of *The Massachusetts Review* that year I had appealed to John Hope Franklin, with whom I had taught at a teachers' retreat in Germany the year before, for advice on black writers and scholars to go after as potential contributors to the journal. Besides Sterling Brown, he named Saunders Redding, who, as it turned out, was scheduled to give a talk at that conference. So there I was, meeting and listening to a fascinating group, including Gwendolyn Brooks, Horace Cayton, Arna Bontemps, Ernest Gaines, Amiri Baraka (then LeRoi Jones), Al Murray. There's a story connected with each of them, but given my focus in these pieces, I will just tell one. Brooks and Jones gave back-to-back readings, and from the floor I had the temerity to ask if there were any significant differences in their poetry. Jones leaped to his feet to denounce me: "That's typical of you white critics, trying to divide us black writers!" My goodness. Rexroth had previously given an impromptu and interesting explanation from the floor of some political background for *Invisible Man* that he had shared in his youth with Ralph Ellison. I think that was the last thing any of us white boys said publicly. Although I will admit that later in the evening Jones invited some of us, sounding very mellow at the door to his smoky and musically vibrant room, to come on in and join the party. I wanted to say, hey, was that your brother who denounced me earlier? But I didn't, and just declined the invitation. We did publish Professor Redding's talk in *MR*.

Nat Hentoff, whom I had known only by reputation when he was a sports writer in Boston, then as a great advocate for press freedom and civil rights, in *The Village Voice* and elsewhere, was a delightful person. He, his wife Margot, and I rented a convertible and drove to Big Sur for lunch one day—great hamburgers—and then an afternoon of wine drinking and conversation at a venerable old poet's mountain house (I have forgotten his name, alas). Wonderful white wine from a gallon jug with him, stunning views, and a memorable comment from Mrs. Hentoff on our way back to Asilomar. As we passed a field of beautiful cows peacefully feeding on the grass, she asked sadly: "You don't think they don't know we are going to kill them?" I was very sorry to hear they divorced some years later.

I ran into Nat shortly thereafter on a street in Greenwich Village. We talked about the conference, and then he asked if I had ever heard Malcolm X. I said something like, oh, he's just one of those marginal extremists who are not significant to the overall Movement. He said, no, he didn't think that way at all, and invited me up to his apartment where he had a tape of Malcolm's speeches. I went, I listened, as did Nat's friend, the artist Maurice Sendak, who had dropped in, and like me listened intently, saying almost nothing. It was the first time I heard Malcolm's voice, or any of his speeches, and it changed my view completely, not to say my life. That man was something, as I was assuredly not the first or last to discover. So I am grateful to Hentoff, who came later on to speak a couple of times at the Valley colleges, where we talked fondly with each other, for contributing to my education in the realities of our time. I forgive him his anti-abortion arguments, too, misguided as I think they are. He remains a champion of human freedom in all other ways.

A further note, in good conscience, about Amiri Baraka, and some other matters: James Baldwin came to our area to teach for three years in the early eighties, and many of us were excited at the prospect of Chinua Achebe, who had also taught at UMass for a semester after the Biafra War, also coming to Amherst at the same time Baldwin was to return in 1987. We had become friends with the Achebes, who had stayed in our house for a short time when we were abroad. They had also lived down the street from us for a while. Now Christie Achebe, Chinua's brilliant wife, was to offer a seminar on African education and women, her doctoral and teaching specialties, at the Humanities Institute I directed at the time. Imagine, two of the great black writers of the world among us, one African American, the other almost universally regarded as "The Father of the Modern African Novel." Then Jimmy died in France, before he could come. We did manage a tribute to him with fine speeches, memories, and tributes, one by Achebe, but it was obviously enveloped by great sorrow.

Baldwin's funeral was held in the Cathedral of St. John the Divine in Manhattan. Anne and I went down to attend it. For some reason we thought it was at Riverside Church, where we went first, only to be instructed otherwise. When we arrived at the entryway of St. John's, finally, we asked a passing priest if this were the place of the James Baldwin memorial service. "No," he said, "This is the place of the funeral service." Well, what is the difference, we who were religiously and ritualistically ignorant, asked somewhat huffily? "At a funeral, the body is there." That hit us in the pit of our stomachs. And, yes, indeed, at the end of the impressive ceremony, begun with intense African drumming that was highly amplified in the Cathedral's soaring vaults, the colorfully garbed Episcopal priests and attendants led the way down the aisle past us with incense and prayers. And behind them the casket with Jimmy's body in it. And behind that the many members of Baldwin's family, his grieving mother in a wheelchair, his brother David, numerous nephews and nieces. The reality of Baldwin as a mortal human being, not just a writer and celebrity, came home to us with terrible force. We never forgot that moment.

Also unforgettable was the eulogy by Amiri Baraka. There had been many tributes by black artists and writers—Maya Angelou, Toni Morrison, Ossie Davis among them, as I remember. Interestingly enough, the only white speaker was the Consul General of France. The audience in the pews, which were filled to capacity, were almost all black people, from many walks of life as far as I could judge. I did not recognize any well-known white writers in attendance—

a sober commentary in itself. But Baraka's speech was the greatest. He had somehow channeled Baldwin into himself as he recounted the life, the works, the signal importance, the voice and tone of James Baldwin. It was amazing and wholly without ego, entirely loving and grateful, and with that I gave up any animus that may have lingered from that silly event a quarter of a century earlier.

I know this postscript breaks with the subject announced in my foreword and the title of this series of sketches. But I felt this was an important story to tell. I have known and/or encountered many other non-Jewish writers, after all, and Baldwin was one of the most memorable, and among the greatest. Sorry if it disturbs the symmetry.

Helen & Jose Yglesias

Actually, I "encountered" Jose Yglesias, Helen's husband of many years, before, sadly, they divorced, and before I met and got to know Helen and her work. Years ago Jerry Liebling, my oldest and dearest friend, reminded me that Jose (no accent over the "e") had written film reviews for *The Daily Worker* for a while in the forties, until he lost the job, presumably because his reviews did not follow the party line, concerned as he was with formal issues as well as content, about which he did not often agree, either. To put this in some kind of perspective, I think it is necessary to give an idea of the period, at least from my worm's eye view. I hope it won't prove a distraction.

I was in high school during the war years, and read the new left-leaning afternoon paper *PM*, avidly. Its editor, Ralph Ingersoll, accompanied my brother's Regular Army New York Regiment, the 16th Infantry, First Division (Leslie had done his basic training on Governor's Island, and came home on weekends in the forties), during the Tunisian campaign, and published pictures of the Battle of El Guettar, a rather remote outpost, but their first battle and victory. How exotic that all sounds now, though it scared the pants off me as much as it thrilled me to know Leslie was there. He had written letters home about the thrill to him, too, of a Jewish Brooklyn boy finding himself in the Atlas Mountains, setting up his platoon's machine guns to ambush those other professional soldiers, from the Afrika Korps. The Germans dropped leaflets denouncing these New York gangster troops, depicting them with Chicago-style tommy guns and with bulbous noses right out of *Der Stuermer*—actually, besides the Jewish volunteers, most of the regiment were Irish and Italian boys, too. It really was, at the outset of the war, a New York regiment, with the sad exception that black troops were not allowed in. That only came in 1947 when President Truman cut the orders (see how easy that could be!) and ended segregation in the Army.

Later, after the defeat at Kasserine Pass—brave but inexperienced troops and officers against an experienced army—and the grim dawn charges up Hill 523 defending the capital city Tunis, where the remnants of his battalion were captured by the Hermann Goering SS Paratroop Division (he and 200 Allied prisoners were subsequently rescued after ten harrowing days) in the final days of the campaign, his tone darkened. He suffered traumatic stress collapse after three days at Gela, the landing beach in Sicily, commanding the lead platoon, fighting off Tiger tanks, and the bloody battle against the cliffs guarding the way to Messina, where the German Army would make their escape to the Italian mainland. There his regiment suffered 50 percent casualties. The horrors of the war were very much with me, even though I played basketball and lusted after girls, too, often feeling guilty about that. The guilt, I suppose, impelled me to write a V-Mail to him every day he was abroad. My brother never chastised me for enjoying life even then; quite the contrary, he approved. He died at the age of 85, bitterly opposed to military brass and war in general, but quite okay about his own life. I presided over his funeral, saying the prayers in Hebrew, as he had over the grave of his best friend, Robert Katz, who had died in the battle of the Kasserine Pass. He described that in a letter to *PM*.

I go on about all this, ancient history as it were, to give the flavor of some of what was going on at the time. So I read *PM*, but not yet *The Worker*, which I began to look at, mostly on Sundays, along with *The New York Times*, and *The Herald-Tribune* (for Red Smith, the great sports writer) when I was in college and beginning to write plays. It seemed to be the thing to do. *PM* had by then folded and become the *Compass*, which I also perused from time to time. Along with *Partisan Review*, Dwight MacDonald's *Politics* (I still have some copies of those journals from that time), *The New Republic* and *The Nation*. From them I heard about European intellectual life, Sartre, Camus, shortly after the war; the challenge of Communism; the struggle for Palestine/Israel. And they had good book reviews.

I didn't discriminate much—forgiving MacDonald for his earlier untenable position on the War (he held to the view that it was primarily an imperialist struggle, and we should stay out of it), or *Partisan's* belated awareness that we had to fight Nazism, as well as Stalinism, and almost none but the Jewish press dealing with the Holocaust. I had learned about that in our neighborhood shul as early as 1943 from European refugees. But those publications did excite discussion and thinking about what road to take after the war: World Federalism? Socialism? Communism? The United Nations? Religion was never on the agenda, except to read and respect Niehbuhr and Tillich, who dealt with moral man in immoral society and religion without God. How different from our world today! If you had asked any of us, of almost any political persuasion, at that time if religion, let alone fundamentalisms, would play any role in the world as we knew it, we would think you had taken leave of your senses.

I got my first smattering of black history, DuBois, Sojourner Truth, Howard Fast's view of Reconstruction (*Freedom Road*), all that, never taught in our schools, from the Communist paper. Also, as well, an appreciation of the suffering of the Russian people and the debt we owed the Red Army, which, as Churchill was to say, "tore the guts out of the German Army." About their winning the war despite Stalin—not because of him—that knowledge would come later and not from them. A rich mix, of the time, towards a rounded education. There was also, of course, the vivid memory of the Depression, which, in 1946, a year that was probably the high point of American communist member-ship, 60 percent of Americans, according to the Gallup Poll, thought it likely we would head into another Depression. So, like almost everyone else I knew, I looked towards the Left for answers, considering myself a socialist, and by my senior year at college, an idealistic, or naïve communist (with a small "c"). No organizational affiliation, except that early in 1947 or 1948 I joined the American Labor Party and dozens of Jewish organizations in picketing the White House in behalf of statehood and recognition for Israel. Then I was one of the 50,000 or so adherents at a Henry Wallace for President rally at Yankee Stadium in 1948, a year before I could actually vote. *Azoy geht es.* That's how it goes—or went.

All of this made me very pleased to get to know Jose and Helen, who also came out of that Old Left background in various ways and shades. They seemed initially more sympathetic types than Phillips, Fiedler, Howe, and other old YPSLs (members of the Young People's Socialist League)—who always seemed so righteous and angry those few years after World War II. I learned to like and listen to them in the fifties and sixties, but later almost all of us relaxed and bonded, as it were. When was that? Perhaps it took the Civil Rights Movement, the Six-Day War in Israel, the 1968 assassinations, the hope for the end of the Vietnam War. I remember a buffet at the Doral in Miami Beach during the McGovern nomination of 1972, where Arthur Miller, Norman Mailer, several Humphrey survivors, Herman Badillo and many others gathered in uneasy unity. The old flames were truly banked a few years later, certainly after the collapse of the Soviet Union. More ancient history, but formative for many of those I am writing about.

Helen became Book Editor of *The Nation* for a few years in the 1960s, after I got to know her, and she gave me the chance to do a couple of book reviews for the journal of which I am rather proud. One on a book about the thirties, in which I got to include a few lines from a fine Stephen Spender poem on the Second World War, and a review essay on Isaac Bashevis Singer, "The Old Jew in New Times," that I think is the one that caught Singer's eye and favor. She also published three novels that I know about, including *Sweetsir* (nice title) and *Family Feeling* (another nice title, but about incest!). She was an immensely kind and generous as well as shrewd literary critic. She had originally asked me to do a collective review of four or five recent novels by young Jewish American writers. I dutifully read them, a struggle, and then said I didn't like any of them and would not write what had to be a negative review of the lot. It was not and is not my style. None were reviewed in *The Nation*. So then she offered me the Singer piece—a game-changing event, as they say.

Jose also was the author of several novels, the first of which, about the people in the cigar wrapping industry of his Cuban American hometown, *A Wake in Ybor City*, is a classic of early American ethnic literature, and just plain good. Many others followed: *Double Double*, *An Orderly Life*, *The Kill Price*, that deal with American life from, by and large, a sophisticated left, Hispanic/New York Jewish (he was not Jewish, but imbibed it!) perspective, in the fifties, sixties and seventies, that are unjustly neglected these days. So are Helen's books. They are both now dead, Jose some years ago, Helen in 2008 in her nineties. And then there is their son, Rafael, who at fifteen wrote his first and beguiling novel, *Hide Fox*, and *All After*, another later called *The Game Player*, with a main Jewish protagonist from suburbia. Quite a family, and not quite living ordinary lives.

I met Jose sometime in 1961–62, when I was in my second year as managing editor of *The Massachusetts Review*. Jose had sent us a piece that I liked at once, his translations of four contemporary Spanish poets more or less covertly anti-Franco, with a short accompanying introduction. I wrote him about it and suggested a sequence for them that he liked and accepted. He also extended an invitation to visit him in New York. I did that, after the publication of his work in an issue of *MR* (Vol. III, No. 2, Winter, 1962) that remains my favorite to this day, among many other memorable issues. It contained a special section on fine blue paper called "A Gathering for William Carlos Williams" (with a cover drawing of Williams by Ben Shahn), and a truly spectacular art insert prepared by Leonard Baskin and Sidney Kaplan on the great Mexican printmaker José (accent over the "e") Guadalupe Posada, printed on thick, gorgeous yellow-orange paper. I had forgotten that Jose's piece, "Four Poets of Spain," appeared right after that Posada insert, and that he was one among an amazing group of other contributors to that number, whom I will not list here. *Où sont les neiges...*

So we met, and he took me to lunch at one of the fashionable and to me fancy restaurants of the day. He was able to do that because he was a well-paid executive of a firm that did business with South America, where his bilingualism was a great asset. Interestingly, he did that job under a pseudonym, which I never learned, while writing and translating under his real name. I'd never encountered that before. We traveled on the subway, where he stood on the platform—tall, movie-star handsome, in a great suit and overcoat—and said he was a like a kid in New York, never getting over his love and fascination with it. He was so alive, vibrant, sunny. Helen had been a nice, soft-spoken Jewish wife married to an English Jew, a serious photographer, with two children.

She left them when she and Jose, a friend of the family for several years and her private writing coach, fell in love and married. Of course they were all free spirits and radicals. Free spirit or not, the former husband, I was told, had a hard time getting over it. In due time the two writers had a son, Rafael, and were happy and very close for many years. They became friends with Leonard and Lisa Baskin and came up to Northampton to visit, where I met Helen.

We all went out one weekend to the Shaker Village in Hancock, got along well, honoring the designs, the honest workmanship and ethical living. We met again when they moved up to Brooklin, Maine to live quietly and write, where they and the Baskins—who had for a time a great estate, as was their wont, with acres of riverfront in Little Deer Isle— visited up and back. On one of those visits, Jose exploded at Leonard for correcting him on the use of some word, Jose shutting Leonard up—a rare occurrence—by shouting that he was the writer, not Leonard. It seemed slightly amusing at the time, but it was a side of him I had not seen before. There was a lot of anger simmering. I suspect the writing, or at least publishing, was not going as well as he and Helen had hoped. Perhaps that was what contributed to the ultimate foundering of the marriage. The long hard winters and isolation were tempered by playing bridge with Mary McCarthy, also living in Maine then. I mentioned earlier that many old political and literary antipathies in that generation had abated—and may have provided some relief. But not enough.

Finally, they sold the place and with the proceeds bought a condo in the Village, a nice apartment that I visited once—

the last time I saw Jose. I did see Helen one more time, when she was in her eighties, already divorced from Jose—still to me a surprising turn of events—at the Coconut Grove Play-house in Miami, where a supposedly new play of Jose's was being performed. She was surrounded by Florida relatives, a group of very obviously elderly Jewish ladies, mostly, and no Jose. The play was not good. It was a throwback to the Ybor City, Tampa days, with a young man, as in an Odets play of the thirties, having to decide whether to join a cigar wrap-pers strike. It was embarrassingly dated, though played with passion and conviction. At the end I didn't know what to say to Helen as we parted. It was the last time I saw either of them—a sad coda to the end of something. Only one more instance of the perennial difficulty of human relationships? Or, towards the end of the last century, the narrowing down of possibility for an earlier generation that had been a hope-ful and socially generous one? The triumph in our time of narcissistic meanness? The end of a dream of transformation and transcendence through politics, art, culture, towards a world more attractive?

It was a dream, I believe, a version of Jacob wrestling with the angel. Even if there was no ladder to a higher and better place, it was a hope that animated so many of the writers I had met and have written about in the foregoing pages.

When Jose died I sent an expression of sympathy and condolence to the family. Many months later I received a call from Rafael, thanking me for that letter. He then added that on the table by the bed in which he died Jose had a copy of *The Massachusetts Review*. Proudly, he had published with us more than that early piece. Lisa Baskin has told me Helen died, at age 92, in an old age home, peaceably, in command to the end of her faculties. I would not have expected less, in our fallen world, from those wonderful people.

Epilogue

A dear old friend and colleague, after reading the fore-going, suggested that I add an epilogue, calling attention to the extraordinary times these people lived through and the faith they kept in sticking to their lasts. A good idea. Especially since many of the writers and other thinkers and critics I encountered over fifty-some years and who left an impression upon me are probably quite unknown to the present generation of readers, even those politically, academically, and ethnically adept. As we are in the second decade of the 21st century, having survived one of the bloodiest, most murderous, yet culturally rich centuries in the history of the West—partially fulfilling and yet denying Spengler's forecast of its twilight—and the dark malignant night of the eight years of Bush-Cheney, it is appropriate to raise a cheer for these artists and thinkers of that time.

Recall that in the 20th century two of the worst wars in history occurred, hundreds of millions killed, maimed, gassed, burned, displaced—World Wars I and II, the second against the most monstrous and inhumane regime ever known. And interminable other horrors, among many, of spilt blood—the Bolshevik Revolution and its consequences, the Spanish Civil War, Fascism, Nazism, Hiroshima and Nagasaki, Vietnam, Korea, Iraq, Israeli-Arab and Palestinian wars, ethnic "cleansings." Closer to home, the Depression of the thirties, the McCarthy period, the pull upon many I have known and chronicled, however briefly, towards, and the repulsion against, the Soviet Union and Communism; Richard Nixon as a prelude to the Bush presidency, one of the worst in American history. Many, if not all, of those I have written about lived through some or most of these events and bore their imprint in their consciousnesses.

In one of Philip Roth's Nathan Zuckerman novels, Zuckerman has to go down to Florida to empty out his recently deceased mother's apartment. He comes upon a sewing kit, and begins to go through it. At the very bottom is a slip of paper, with a single word on it: "Holocaust." "I didn't know she knew the word," Nathan says. Yes, she did. As does every Jew, even the most assimilated, non-identifying. It's there, somewhere in the recesses of one's consciousness or unconsciousness. The same is true of any thinking person who went through the period of those other horrors, as part, on some level, of their own histories and stories.

Even as they tried to be true to "art," or their critical calling, and not be overtly tendentious, they kept writing, thinking, acting politically, or in a less loaded terminology, were responsible to the realities of their time and condition. They tried to comprehend or countermand, directly or obliquely, these momentous events and their effect upon the irreducibly human. One might recall Allen Ginsberg's line during one of our wars: "Okay, Uncle Sam, I'll put my queer shoulder to the wheel!"

I like the implicit irony in that. As if to say he understood how ineffectual literary actions might be, how vulnerable and often marginal and suspect most artists may be, as they sought the right word, sentence, line, image. Yet they will make the effort to address the issues of their time, as those impinged on them. These acts are important to us all, however little effect they may seem to have had or the evanescence and loss of those efforts in the shrouds of history and forgetfulness. At the least they should remind us that we are all in this together, whatever our age, politics, sex or sexual preferences, race and ethnicity.

I think, too, about something I mentioned briefly in the piece on Irving Howe. I admired the title of one of his books: *Steady Work*, which is a reference to a Sholem Aleichem story about Chelm, the mythical East European Jewish town of fools. In the story the narrator comes upon a tall tower at the edge of town, in which the town beggar sits. "What are you doing up there?" "I'm hired by the town to watch for the coming of the Messiah, and to yell out to them when it happens." "What can they pay you for such a job?" "Not very much, but it's steady work." And indeed it is steady work—work that many of the writers and critics I've encountered and dealt with were also doing—and frequently for not very much earthly reward. They struggled to keep the faith, as it were, in a better world, more generous and just than what they and we have to live with. Through art, literature, criticism, culture generally, they tried to keep alive the idea and hope of a world more attractive—as Trotsky called literature—often in the worst of times. I even include people with whose politics and ideas I often disagreed—and all those who kept going through bad times and good, on the margin or very occasionally at the center of the literary world. All, trying to transcend the sordid and the selfish, the narcissistic, as best they could. Even in themselves. None of us is an angel. Let us praise them all, the famous and the infamous. Those in this memoir, and those many others not mentioned in these pages. To them this modest work is dedicated.

Amherst, 2012

Photo by Ned Gray

About the Author

Jules Chametzky is Professor of English, emeritus, at the University of Massachusetts Amherst, where he taught from 1958 until 2004. He was a founder of *The Massachusetts Review*, of which he is Editor, emeritus, after 27 years as senior co-editor. He was born May 24, 1928 in Brooklyn, and attended Brooklyn Technical High School, Brooklyn College (B.A., 1950) and the University of Minnesota (M.A., 1952; Ph.D., 1958). He has taught at the University of Minnesota and Boston University, and as a Fulbright or guest professor at the Free University of Berlin and six other European universities. Chametzky has published numerous articles and reviews on Jewish American and American literature in popular and academic journals. He was president of the Association of Literary Magazines (ALMA) and then secretary of the Executive Committee of the Coordinating Council of Literary Magazines (CCLM). His major publications include *From the Ghetto: The Fiction of Abraham Cahan*; *Our Decentralized Literature: Cultural Mediations in Selected Jewish and Southern Writers*; and the Penguin edition of Abraham Cahan's *The Rise of David Levinsky*. He co-edited *Black and White in American Culture: Ten Years of The Massachusetts Review*; and *Jewish American Literature: A Norton Anthology*. Chametzky is the father of three sons and was married for 52 years to the late poet Anne Halley.